ASATRU
FOR BEGINNERS

The Ultimate, Modern Approach to Norse Paganism, Heathenry, their Gods and Rituals to Understanding and Integrating Ásatrú into Your Life

JAYDEN K. HELMAN

TABLE OF CONTENTS

INTRODUCTION

The term Asatru, used to describe the indigenous religion of Europe, is Old Norse and derives from two words, *Asa* which is one of the classes of Nordic Gods, and *tru* which means to be true, loyal, or to be 'in troth' with. Hence, the term *Asatru* means to be true to the Aesir Gods. The term Asatru has become the dominant and prevailing term used to describe the indigenous Nordic religion which refers to the Aesir deities.

Although Asatru is a sort of personal religion, it is also about ancestor worship, praying, dancing, and chanting together. It is about drinking consecrated mead together, and it is about worshipping and calling on the gods as a community. Therefore, it is important that you find your Heathen kindred and become part of it.

Also, the more you connect with other Pagans, the more you learn about your faith, and the deeper your beliefs get. Being part of a kindred is immensely useful in your research about your religion. Moreover, when other believers share their experiences with you, you will realize how similar these experiences are to your own.

It gives you a sense of identity and makes you realize and accept the presence of gods and deities all around you. You are able to counter arguments about being crazy to believe in the existence of gods. You know and accept their existence without question because you know others have had the same experiences as you.

Asatru does carry a rich tapestry of tradition, history, legends, myths, symbolism, and rituals, aspects that can also be described as religious in nature.

The Asatru adherents refer to themselves as Asatruar and prefer a reconstructionist approach in their practices. It is a community-based path, so any Asatruar acts for the good of the community. One of the best things about Asatru is that it is a great private religion. You can be an Astruar, and no one else needs to know about your beliefs but you. You are free to choose what attracts you to Asatru. And yet, numerous kindred groups all over the world offer you a sense of identity and connection with other practicing Asatruars. In the last chapter, you'll discover how to contact practitioners in your area and even learn how to start your own hearth.

Asatru is a modern Icelandic term that is related specifically to the worship and veneration of the Aesir gods. Asatru is a term that is used often in formal settings among the Asatru community, more often than Norse Paganism or Heathenism. Although followers of Asatru know and believe in the Vanir gods, they don't talk about or worship any other deities but those from the Aesir tribe. Some believe that Vanatru is a direct outcome of the lack of involvement and engagement by the Asatruar with the Vanir deities.

Asatru has a fairly rigid and formalized set of rules to follow. The things that are expected of you as a follower of that faith could lead to a large formal community that follows the belief system. On the other hand, Heathenism and Norse Paganism seek small-scale communities that are self-sufficient in each of their traditions, cultures, and belief systems.

One of the most important things to know about Asatru is that there is no missionary or proselytizing events that happen. People can join the community if they want. There is nothing given in return for becoming a Heathen. You do it only if it is your calling.

This book contains that kind of information too, such as how to practice Asatru on your own, as well as how to find other practitioners and be part of a like-minded kindred group. The hands-on instructions on how to practice this belief system at home will give you sufficient material to start off immediately, even as you prepare yourself to become part of something larger.

This book is a primer on all the practices and beliefs Asatruars follow. If you've ever been interested in the history of Asatru, then read on.

Criticisms

Just like any other religion, people have attempted to modify Asatru to meet their own agendas. Asatru was revitalized by the Europeans to connect back with their roots and not to establish their supremacy over other racial groups. However, the Asatru faith has been misused time and time again by white supremacists to divide the people of the world.

Many white supremacy groups use symbols from Asatru texts like the Eddas. White supremacists believe that Asatru is the best tool to prove themselves superior because they think this religion symbolizes European prowess.

None of these supremacy movements have emerged from

Asatru, and most of them don't even have proper knowledge about the beliefs held sacred by the Asatruars. The vast majority of Asatruars claim to have nothing to do with any white supremacy groups and they don't believe in the ideology of one group dominating the other. According to the Asatruars, not every person of white descent belongs to their group either. Only those whose ancestors were of pagan faith are invited to follow this path because it's a spiritual philosophy more suited to them.

We have discussed the history of Asatru and how it almost disappeared from the face of the earth. We also saw how Asatru has been on the rise in recent years throughout the world. The influence of Asatru isn't visible only in Northern Europe, but even in the USA, where many people are adopting it rapidly.

CHAPTER 1

What Is Asatru?
Why Is It So Popular?

Defined by the belief in the ancient Norse gods, Asatru is also referred to as *heathenry* and its practitioners are called *heathens*. It is a modern Neopagan belief that has its foundation in the pre-Christian religions of Scandinavia and Northern Europe.

Asatru is a modern spirituality based on the traditions, folklore, and mythology of Northern Europe and particularly Scandinavia. Around 1,000 years ago, Scandinavians and other peoples in Northern Europe converted to Christianity but, for many, the gods and spirits of the old pre-Christian religions were still important. People continued to tell stories about them and, in some ways, continued to venerate them. Eventually, some of the stories about the ancient gods and spirits were written down by historians and antiquarians, who were interested in preserving knowledge about the past. These texts have since been used in modern times to revive a spirituality centered around the Norse gods.

Asatru is a modern Icelandic word that was originally used by Danish scholars in the 19*th* century when referring to the pre-Christian religion in Scandinavia. In its Danish and Swedish forms, it is spelled *asatro*, and in Norwegian, it is spelled *åsatru*. The Scandinavians all pronounce the word differently, but in English, the Icelandic way of saying it would phonetically sound like *ow-sa-troo*. The word is a combination of the Norse word *áss* (god, spirit. Plural: *æsir*) and the word *trú* (belief). Asatru means *belief in the æsir*, and people who believe in the æsir can be referred to as Asatruar, with the Icelandic plural suffix—*ar* at the end of the word. The word came into use in the English language, especially in the United States, in the 1970s, under influence of Iceland. In modern English, most heathens use it in the sense "belief in the æsir," but some also emphasize *trust* in the æsir.

Though Asatru is an ancient language, it was near extinct after Christianization hit Europe. Many were forced to follow a different religion and the ancient ways nearly disappeared.

However, they made a comeback in the 1970s as the revival of Germanic Paganism was celebrated once more. In Iceland, on the Summer Solstice of 1972, it was recognized as an official religion once again. Shortly after, Asatru groups formed in the United States.

The religion is similar to the ancient ways of Norse culture, before Christianity.

Asatru is "true to the Aesir." Asatruars believe that gods are living beings who take an active role in the world. Much of the Asatru beliefs are based on Old Norse mythology. There are three types of deities within Asatru: the Aesir, the Vanir, and the Jotnar. The Aesir is the primary focus of worship of the deities, though worshipping the other two branches is also accepted. Some of the gods and goddesses include:

- Odin, the one-eyed father figure who learned secret wisdom by hanging from Yggdrasil for nine nights.
- Frigg, the wife of Odin and goddess of marriage and motherhood with a talent for divinity and 'seeing.'
- Freyr and Freya, the brother and sister deities of fertility, love, and battle.

- Thor, Odin's son and the god of thunder who wields a divine hammer.
- Loki, the trickster god who has, on numerous occasions, shown a lack of honor.

These gods were just a few among the many gods of the Aesir. There are also a number of gods among the Vanir and Jotnar that Asatru followers may worship, though the focus should be primarily on the Aesir gods.

Asatru also believes in the Nine Noble Virtues, Norse Paganism's version of the Ten Commandments. As with many things in Norse mythology, the sacred number nine appears. These virtues are the basic Norse standards of courage, honor, discipline, industriousness, hospitality, self-reliance, perseverance, truth, and fidelity.

The Asatru Association

The Asatru Association is an Icelandic religious formalized organization of Heathenry established on the First Day of Summer in 1972 by Sveinbjörn Beinteinsson, a farmer and poet. The First Day of Summer in Iceland is a national holiday and is celebrated on the first Thursday after April 18th every year. The Asatru Association was recognized and registered as a religious organization in 1973. The chief religious official or the highest office of the Asatru Association is referred to as "Allsherjargodi," an elected post.

The priests in Asatru are called Godi, and each Godi is given a congregation called godord to work with. While each godord is more or less connected to certain geographic regions, there is no compulsion to join any specific godord. You are free to join any congregation that you like.

The legal approval allowed the organization to conduct legally binding rituals and ceremonies, as well as to collect a share of the church tax, which is imposed by the tax on religious congregations to run and manage churches and their employees. Sveinbjörn Beinteinsson led this organization from its inception in 1972 until his death in 1993. During his time, the membership of this organization did not exceed 100 people, and there was not much activity.

The second Allsherjargodi was Jörmundur Ingi Hansen, who led the organization from 1994 to 2002, and it was during this time that the Asatru Association witnessed considerable activity and growth. The third and current leader is the musician Hilmar Örn Hilmarsson, who took charge in 2003.

Asatru does not conform to a fixed religion, theology, or dogma. Each individual is free to have his or her own beliefs. For example, many Wiccan members are also members of the Asatru Association. The Asatru priests believe in a pantheistic perspective. The communal blot feast is the central ritual of Asatru. The priests also conduct naming ceremonies called gooar, weddings, funerals, coming of age, and other rituals too.

Asatru Perspectives

The modern Asatru/Heathenism community has three primary perspectives, namely, Universalism, Folkism, and Tribalism. Of these three, the first two perspectives are the main ones, while the third, Tribalism, takes a middle-ground approach.

Universalism—According to the people who believe in this

perspective, anyone from any background can become a Heathen. A Universalist perspective offers more freedom of choice to everyone, even while giving greater options for Heathenism to grow and expand its reach across the globe.

Folkism—The Folkish perspective believes that Asatru is an ethnic religion and entry should be restricted only to those with a North European heritage. This belief of Folkism is based on the idea that ethnic religions connect followers to the local landscape, bloodline, ancestors, and traditions. So, outsiders can't find a connection with the ethnic elements and will fail to be genuine practitioners.

Tribalism—Folkism and Universalism are at the two ends of the Asatru spectrum, while those who follow Tribalism take a middle stand. They accept and embrace the Folkish stand of the need for a deep connection and feeling for Norse culture to be able to call oneself an Asatru. Surface-level adoption of Asatru principles is not enough. A person can be inducted into the clan in one of two ways, specifically if he or she is of Germanic origin or if the person is converted, adopted, or takes an oath into the community.

Just like any other religion, people have attempted to modify Asatru to meet their own agendas. Asatru was revitalized by the Europeans to connect back with their roots and not to establish their supremacy over other racial groups. However, the Asatru faith has been misused time and time again by white supremacists to divide the people of the world.

Many white supremacy groups use symbols from Asatru texts like the Eddas. White supremacists believe that Asatru is the best tool to prove themselves superior because they think this religion symbolizes European prowess.

None of these supremacy movements have emerged from Asatru, and most of them don't even have proper knowledge about the beliefs held sacred by the Asatruars. The vast majority of Asatruars claim to have nothing to do with any white supremacy groups and they don't believe in the ideology of one group dominating the other. According to the Asatruars, not every person of white descent belongs to their group either. Only those whose ancestors were of pagan faith are invited to follow this path because it's a spiritual philosophy more suited to them.

Even the Nazis tried to misuse Asatru under the reign of Adolf Hitler by twisting and contorting the Asatru beliefs to match their own racist agenda. This came to an end after World War II when the Germans were defeated, but some neo-Nazi groups throughout the world are again trying to resurrect the disdainful beliefs of Aryan supremacy. It would be wrong to accuse an entire religion of being racist, and if it's being done, it can lead to a similar phenomenon like the Islamophobia that's currently

CHAPTER 2

ASATRU VALUES

prevailing in the entire world.

Courage

The Asatru defines courage as an element of pagan virtue that drives an individual to act and behave in the right way, even in the absence of reward or in the face of certain defeat. This definition clearly emerged in all the Norse stories and legends. The powerful monsters are central to all Norse mythological themes, but they were not given an honorable character.

Contrarily, the heroes found potent solutions to kill the monsters driven by sheer courage and willpower. In fact, the concept of courage being paramount in a person's life is the reason, however misplaced, that gave rise to the opinions that the Vikings were godless.

The Viking people were so focused on their courage to do the right thing that they believed that martial heroism was a power of its own. In today's world, courage is more than martial bravery. It also means to stand up for the right thing. For example, turning into a whistleblower when the company you work for has violated laws is considered to be a courageous thing to do, according to the Asatru.

Norse Paganism believed that courage was all about having faith and trust in your own strength. Courage, according to

Asatru, also includes being brave to live according to the Nine Noble Virtues. Asatruars believe that it is vital to stand up in a hostile world to be counted among the true and authentic people of character.

Honor

Honor is all about the value of recognizing and accepting nobility, both within and outside of us. Honor is not only your own feeling of self-worth rooted in your noble character but also showing respect to others. Perhaps honor is one of the most difficult virtues to define because different people can interpret it differently.

The importance of living an honorable life is contained in this small proverb in the *Poetic Edda,* "Everything and everyone in this world dies. However, the reputation of dead people never dies." So, good or bad deeds survive even after our deaths, and they carry the glory or burden of our soul.

Truth

There are two types of truth: spiritual and actual. Spiritual truth is what you know to be true spiritually and personally. Many describe their belief in god as a spiritual truth; something they just know, without 'proof.'

The actual truth is just as it sounds; it's the truth. As they say, honesty is the best policy. It can be hard to be honest, especially if it's something that you know that someone doesn't want to hear. It's why you lie when your friend asks if they look good in those pants—you don't want to hurt their feelings. However, the consequences of telling the truth, such as a bruised ego, are far less than the consequences of lying.

Truth and courage go hand in hand. Without truth, you have no courage to stand up for your beliefs because you don't know your beliefs to be true. How are you going to root for something you feel ho-hum about? It goes the other way, too. You need courage to speak the truth. Especially when it means hurting someone you care about.

Although speaking the truth is always encouraged, there are times it can be damaging. Don't be fooled into speaking the truth you hear from others if they are dishonest. It may be unintentional, but you're spreading lies and that's worse than saying nothing. In fact, if you don't know for certain the truth that you speak, you shouldn't say anything.

Truth also correlates with living a virtuous life. Generally, when you lie it's because you're trying to avoid punishment for wrongdoing. Lead a morally positive life and you have no reason to feel tempted to lie.

Discipline

Discipline, or more accurately self-discipline, is also an extremely critical value to stand by. Mastering this will give you the opportunity to uphold the other virtues as well. Properly reinforced personal discipline will provide you with the ability to stand up for your truths, your moral code, and much more. Upholding these virtues has to be your choice, which you will only be able to make if you are strong enough to do so. If you are, you can face any challenge, whether it's a personal goal to conquer or ignoring what everyone expects you to do.

With all the temptations lurking around in our modern societies and all the people who would like to exercise their own will over us, keeping up your standards can be challenging. It takes years and years to master the perfect self-discipline, but it's certainly worth it. It means you won't have to adhere to something you absolutely don't want to or don't believe in. In addition, it can teach you how to avoid unnecessary complications in life. One way to do this is by having the discipline to put your faith in yourself. By doing this, you will be less likely to rely on other means for emotional support, and you will become a much stronger individual.

Hospitality

Hospitality is the sense of service you have. It reflects your willingness to share what you have with your people and community. Of course, this does not mean that you mindlessly give away everything you have to anyone who comes knocking at your door. Hospitality is about sharing and giving and has a reciprocity effect as well.

When guests come to your house, it is your duty to make them as comfortable as you can and to offer them food and drink. Hospitality is a very important virtue in Asatru: their gods travel all over the cosmos, including to Midgard or the realm of human beings. With that in mind, a guest in your house could be a god in disguise, and it is your duty to honor him or her.

Also, hospitality drives a sense of readiness to help and assist people in need. It drives interdependence in the community and forges strong bonds among the members. In fact, for ancestors, hospitality was not just a virtue, it was a necessity.

In those days, traveling long distances posed a lot of difficulties and was also dangerous. Yet, traveling was important for trade and commerce. So, Norsemen and women of those times freely opened their homes not only to their friends and other known tribespeople but also to strangers.

People who came knocking would be provided with a warm place to rest their tired feet, warm food to fill their bellies, and even warm clothes to wear. In return, the guest was expected to eat moderately, entertain their hosts with songs and stories, and give little gifts such as small trinkets. Havamal talks about the importance of hospitality in the following way: "A guest who has traveled needs the warmth of a fire for his numb knees, warm water to wash, clean clothes and food to fend off the hunger and cold."

Self-Reliance

Any of these Nine Noble Virtues can be mastered if you decide to take the matter into your own hands. And while the Norse gods could provide you with some general guidance in life, you should be able to rely on yourself more to make any life-altering decisions. You are the only one who has the power to change your life and make better decisions for yourself. And of course, you will only be able to do this if you take care of yourself, in body and mind. This way, you can also avoid unjustly blaming everything and anything for your mishaps and take responsibility for your actions.

Now when it comes to self-reliance, sometimes you will have to find a balance between relying on your own instinct and asking for the guidance of others. If you don't learn how to thrive as an individual, you won't be able to help do the same in your community. Additionally, you may want to avoid only doing things for others so you can get something back. By being able to rely on yourself, you will free your mind of materialism and other temptations as well. Norse people were not too reliant on the value of material possessions either; they appreciated possessions for their existence and purpose in their lives.

Industriousness

This virtue is all about your willingness to work hard at all times and to strive for efficiency. The trick is in seeing the journey of industriousness as a joyous activity. It is imperative that we work hard to achieve our goals, to find what we seek. Without hard work and perseverance, we can never reach our goals.

And yet, working hard without time to relax and enjoy your life is also not the Asatru way. Industriousness is a virtue that has hard work at its core, but it also means you take pride in your work. Asatru's definition of industriousness goes a little above and beyond too. The value system of Asatru says this about industriousness: "Unless you are disabled, a full-time student, or already employed, it is your duty to find a job and do it diligently."

If you have a problem finding a job, then endeavor to find some like-minded people and start a venture. Asatruars believe that without work, there can be no self-worth. We cannot provide for our families. We cannot achieve our goals or strive to reach perfection in our lives. Being lazy is one of the worst lessons you can teach your children.

Industriousness also means striving hard for self-improvement. We should not be happy with mediocrity or working in a way that simply helps us to survive. Our industriousness should drive us to achieve greater efficiency and productivity and to thrive in our lives. This virtue is specifically useful in the modern era where life has become very convenient. It is easy to go to a grocery store, come home, put some ingredients together, and create a meal for yourself, unlike the ancient times when there was a lot of work to do, such as cows to milk, fields to till, cattle to feed, and much more, before food was ready to be eaten. Thus, industriousness was a necessity to prevent starvation.

Today, laziness may not result in starvation, but it does cause a lot of other problems, including joblessness and a total loss of self-worth, without which your life can be a living hell. Self-reliance and industriousness work hand in hand. Your sense of independence will drive you to do your work without depending on anyone. This approach drives you to work hard. You don't wait for things to be done by others, and you don't wait for your life to be handed over to you on a platter.

Perseverance

It's simple: don't give up, no matter how hard life gets. You will continually get knocked down, but failure isn't what matters, what matters is trying. So, did you make a mistake? Learn from your mistakes and move on. In the process, you've gained insight into something you would never have known if you had not failed.

When you think of people you admire, who comes to mind?

Generally, someone who's worked hard to get what they want. You don't root for someone who quits easily or is handed everything; you root for the person who never gives up, even when they think they've lost it all.

Fidelity

This is one of the most complex virtues any human being can possess. Fidelity can be interpreted as staying true to your faith, your personal relationships, or your community. And all of these have the same importance in one's life, which is why upholding this value could make you the best individual you can be. In the times of the ancient Norse folk, this was almost entirely a question of faith in gods. Breaking an oath was equal to offending a god, and more than once, it was known to have led to physical confrontations. Furthermore, many followers of Norse paganism still tie every other aspect of fidelity to this primal one.

While modern society does not believe that it is possible to keep one's word anymore, staying true to your faith could open up a door for a rewarding future. After all, if people know you are faithful, they will trust you. And this is true even for people who only know one aspect of your life. If they know you stick

CHAPTER 3

HISTORY OF ASATRU

to your word in one regard, they will be reassured that you will stick to it in all others as well. This will strengthen all your relationships and help you create much more.

The Asatru movement can be traced as far back as the 1970s, when a wave of revival swept across the entire religious landscape. Germanic paganism was gaining traction, and people began to realize the importance of their old faiths. Everything took a concrete shape when the Íslenska Ásatrúarfélagið was founded on the first day of Summer Solstice in 1972. Also known as the Icelandic Fellowship of the Aesir Faith, this organization was among the first to actually kick off the Neopagan movement.

The "Asatru Free Assembly" also came to be established in the USA soon after, and they later became the "Asatru Folk Assembly." This marked the spread of the Asatru faith throughout the world rather than being limited to the European continent. The spread of this old faith was cemented by the efforts of various individuals throughout the world. The "Asatru Alliance" has been holding an annual gathering of all its followers known as "The Althing" for over 25 years and customs like these are what keep this faith spreading.

Asatru is a modern pagan religion founded early in the 20th century, but it was only later that it managed to get recognition from the Scandinavian governments. In 1972, the Icelandic religious organization, Ásatrúarfélagið (Asatru Fellowship), was created. A year after, it was given legal recognition as a religious institute. While the religion seems newly formed, it is deeply rooted in the Germanic religions that came before

Christianity. A more accurate term to describe Asatru would be "a reconstruction." Asatru is based on one of the religions practiced in Scandinavia, the Netherlands, France, England, and the rest of Northern Europe in the period preceding the arrival of Christianity. In other words, it isn't technically a newly formed religion but rather a revival of old traditions.

In Ancient Norse, Asatru means "belief in the Aesir." The Aesir being the Norse Gods. Because the religion was practiced across such a large region in the past, it acquired many names. Vanatrú, Forn Sed, Vor Sir, Forn Sir, Odinism, Wodenism, Nordisk Sed, and more. In English, it is known as Norse or Germanic Heathenism. While it is also known as Neopaganism, this is not accurate a preferred one by the practitioners, known as the Asatruars.

The foundation of Asatru lies in a number of Norse myths documented in ancient scripts, mainly the Poetic and Prose Eddas. As for the rituals, traditions, and values, these were explained and described in sagas and some surviving texts. Keep in mind, the Asatruar don't necessarily believe in the myths being historically accurate, and neither do they believe in the literal execution of some outdated rituals, like blood sacrifices. However, they do believe in the values and the way of living that the rituals and myths represented. Yet, the matter is much more complicated than that.

From its origins as a folk religion, Norse paganism went through a long journey to reach the whole of Northern Europe. Not just that, but religion also faced the threat of growing empires. It went from a place of massive popularity to become a hidden faith due to prosecution. Eventually, Norse paganism reached a point where it was almost completely extinguished. How the Asatru religion was reconstructed until it assumed its current form today, we can only understand that by looking back at the origins of the Old Norse religion, which planted the seed for Asatru.

The world has started going back to its roots. The things that were once considered old-fashioned and outdated by the previous generations are adopted happily by younger minds. Living modestly was once a virtue until it became obsolete, and it's made a comeback yet again. Growing one's own food was also the norm a long time ago until industrialization happened and it's back again as well. Similarly, the religious ideas that were once discarded have started to resurface once again.

Many people throughout the Scandinavian countries and the rest of the world are turning back to Asatru as the answer to everything. This ancient religion dates back to the times when Christianity or the Jewish faith hadn't even taken shape. Call them "Heathens" or "Asatruar," the followers of this faith believe in going back to the old ways of their ancestors.

Asatru is actually a modern term and not a traditionally used word, unlike what most people believe. Basically, the origin of the word "Asatru" lies in the Danish "Asetro," which roughly translates to heathenism. The meaning of Asatru can be understood by separating its component words Asa and Tru. After dissecting the word into two parts, we can understand that it means "belief in the gods."

It was first used in 1885 in an article, and then it was used again in 1945. Some sources also claim that the modern rendition of heathenism in the form of "Asatru" was first used in 1873 as a part of Edvard Grieg's opera called "Olav Trygvason." The exact origins of this word are debatable, and different scholars have different theories.

There are various other terms used for heathenism like "Heidni" and "Forn Sidr." These are old terms that were used traditionally in the Old Norse language. Some people also call it "Odinism" because of the primary emphasis on the god Odin, who's considered the king of gods. However, "Odinism" has taken on a more negative connotation in the recent past due to the popularity of this word among white supremacy groups. We'll be discussing this issue further in this chapter, and we'll explore what the actual practitioners of Asatru feel about this issue.

The exact age of this religion is not very clear either, but it's widely accepted that Asatru, in its original form, is much older than Christianity, Buddhism, and many other religions. Some people claim that Asatru could be almost as old as Hinduism, if not older. Asatru has also shown some Paleolithic characteristics like shamanism and some Neolithic features like the concepts of "honor" and "shame."

Asatru was slowly replaced by Christianity in the primarily dominant region of Iceland. The settlers from Iceland were influenced by Christian beliefs as they traveled to Europe, and some of them brought home their new beliefs. This caused a divide between the people who followed Christianity and those who followed Asatru. In order to handle this divide and stop the nation from splitting, the parliament of the Viking commonwealth decided to make Christianity the only religion of Iceland. The followers of the old ways continued their practices in secret, but slowly, Christianity took over.

The last bastion of paganism fell when Lithuania officially converted to Christianity in 1386. This marked the end of paganism in Europe, but the Indo-European gods continued to survive in other regions. India, for example, was one of those places where the pagan gods were still thriving. The pagan gods had their Vedic counterparts who were greatly similar in detail. Thor became Indra, Odin became Rudra, and so on.

Even though Asatru was almost completely replaced, it resurfaced in the modern era and started to attract more people. We will be looking at the emergence of Asatru and how it's becoming one of the fastest-growing religions in Iceland today. We will also look into the different aspects of Asatru's history and the traditional beliefs that Asatru and its followers hold dear.

The Asatruars believe their modern version of this religion is identical to the practices of their ancestors. This Neopaganism tries to emulate all the practices and beliefs of their ancestors and followers believe Asatru blends all the positive attributes from both the older tradition and the newer culture which comes together to create something that resounds with the believers.

Almost every Asatruar will give you a similar answer when you ask them where they gained their insight from—the Norse Eddas. Since most of the religion was purged by the Christians who labeled the pagans as barbarians, there isn't a lot of content other than the Eddas left. Another credible source of information for those who reconstructed the pagan religion is folktales. These tales have been preserved since time immemorial and have been passed on from one generation to the other.

For the first time in centuries, the practice of the Asatru and heathen faith has emerged and has begun to gain prevalence. While not a globally recognized faith, the number of practitioners has increased in recent years.

While there isn't a set reason for this, I'd like to believe that it is because the world has become more accepting of difference and change in recent years. Global society is less stuck in its ways than it once was.

This shift in perspective has allowed Asatru to once again flourish. But, where did Asatru come from? And how has it managed to grow in popularity over the years?

Asatru is a modern attempt to revive the ancient Norse faith that originated in Northern Europe. It aims to revive, reconstruct, and reimagine the ancient faith (*Asatru*, n.d.). The history of Northern European polytheism stretches back as far as the Bronze Age and Viking Age. During this period, variations of the faith developed among the German, British, and Nordic countries (*Asatru*, n.d.).

While these faiths faced harsh persecution once the Christian faith grew in power, it has reemerged.

Asatru emerged in the early 1970s and was 'founded' by an Icelandic farmer by the name of Sveinbjörn Beinteinsson (1924–1993). In 1972, he petitioned the Islandic government to recognize the Íslenska Ásatrúarfélagið (Icelandic fellowship of Æsir faith) as a legitimate religious faith. He achieved this goal in 1973, the following year (*History of Asatru—ReligionFacts*, 2005).

Later, the countries of Denmark and Norway followed suit.

In addition to Denmark and Norway, the Asatru Free Assembly was formed in the US, and later, this title was changed to the Asatru Folk Assembly (*Asatru*, n.d.).

The word Asatru stems from the modern Islandic 'Æsir Faith.' Therefore, Asatru centers around one of the major tribes of Norse deities known as the Aesir.

At the time of writing this, Asatru has become Iceland's largest non-Christian religion. Asatru has also flourished in the United States, and in 2017, the Department of Defense officially recognized the Asatru. This allowed practitioners their full religious rights in all service branches (*Asatru*, n.d.).

Modern Norse Paganism

Modern Norse Paganism (Asatru) was established in the 1970s. It was recognized as a religion by the Icelandic state in 1973. The poet Sveinbjörn Beinteinsson along with eleven other Icelanders lobbied the Icelandic government about recognizing Asatru as a religion after establishing a formal congregation. It is unclear whether the group were practitioners of the Old Norse religion or just studying it, but they succeeded in their task either way. Those 12 people then held a meeting on the First Day of Summer, an important pagan holiday that denotes the end of winter and the beginning of summer.

Beinteinsson, along with his small congregation, was a key

figure in getting modern Norse Paganism recognized by the Icelandic government. The association that formed in the process was Ásatrúarfélagið, "the fellowship of those who are true to the gods," although it is often just referred to as Asatru. It is currently Iceland's most common and fastest growing non-Christian religion. Since its recognition as an official religion, Modern Norse Pagan organizations began to sprout all around the Western world. In the United States, Robert Stine and Stephen McNallen formed the Viking Brotherhood, later renamed "Asatru Folk Alliance." The Department of Defense officially recognized Asatru/Heathenry in 2017 that resulted in giving full religious rights to Heathens in every service branch.

In Great Britain, the Committee for the Restoration of the Odinic Rite was founded by John Yeowell and others. Since these three were the first recognized Modern Norse Pagan organizations, the interest in the faith kept growing with other associations and organizations emerging and introducing new approaches and ideas. There are currently around twenty thousand Norse Pagans worldwide.

The Beliefs

The Asatruars believe that divine beings can be divided into different categories. We'll be discussing the different divine beings and other mythological creatures in great detail in the upcoming chapters. In this section, we'll only be briefly looking at the different categories of creatures that the Asatruar believe in.

There are Aesirs, who are the gods worshipped by the pagans and the neopagans. The Aesir are usually characterized as benevolent, strong, valiant, and as a good force. While the Vanir are considered to be indirectly related to the Aesir clan and represent natural elements like nature and earth. Lastly, there are the Jotnar and these are giants who are always opposed to the Aesir.

The Aesir and the Jotnar are always engaged in war, and the Jotnar are symbolized as exact opposites of the Aesir. This doesn't mean there aren't any exceptions since there have been a few giants who actually cooperated with the gods, and a few giantesses have even borne the children of some gods.

The Asatruars also believe that those who lead a righteous life and die valiantly in battle will be rewarded in the afterlife. These people are supposedly escorted by the Valkyries led by Freyja to Valhalla. The fallen warriors get to join Odin, leader of the gods, and feast on a pig called Särimner. Särimner is slaughtered, eaten, and resurrected each day. Similarly, the warriors feast in Valhalla and go out to battle daily with Odin as well.

While the brave feast in Valhalla, cowards, and immoral men go to Hifhel, which is a place meant for tormenting the wicked. However, those who are the opposite, neither valiant nor immoral end up in a place called Hel. This Hel in Norse mythology isn't akin to the hell in Abrahamic faiths. Hel is a place of perpetual calm and peace, much like limbo.

Every Viking used to live by a code that dictated what they should and shouldn't do. The modern Astruars have a similar code as well and this code helps them walk a righteous path in life without deviating to any sinful ways. These "Nine Noble Virtues" that are followed by the modern Asatruars are listed below:

- Courage
- Truth
- Honor
- Fidelity
- Discipline
- Hospitality
- Industriousness
- Self-Reliance
- Perseverance

These virtues have only been mentioned here to give you a general idea about the values that are cherished by the Asatruars. The Asatru beliefs are very different when compared to the other Abrahamic religions. The Asatruars worship many gods, and their religion is polytheistic; this is a belief that's much less extreme since Asatru doesn't undermine the validity of gods from other religions either. However, according to Christianity, there is a trinity composed of God, the father, Jesus, his son, and the Holy Spirit who reign supreme as one. Christians believe that there are a fixed number of realms, and all of those are ruled by one God only. The Islamic beliefs also refute the existence of any other god besides Allah, and they discard the beliefs of any other religions as well.

This is why there can be no conquests and crusades as Asatru doesn't try to impose itself on anyone. The people of North European descent can choose to follow the Asatru faith since they are direct descendants of the ones who practiced paganism before the Christians converted the majority of the world to their faith.

Asatru isn't very clear or definitive on the afterlife either. While the Abrahamic faiths believe in a place called heaven for the righteous and a burning hell for the sinners, Asatru interprets death entirely differently. The Hel that exists in Norse paganism is nothing but a place of calm and peace where the dead aren't tormented like in Hell.

However, those who commit grave sins and who are considered the lowest of the low are taken to Nastrond. It's a place of eternal punishment for the ones who lead an immoral life and don't uphold the virtues as mentioned in the "Nine Noble Virtues." The severity of a crime has to be very high to be sent to this place and only the most heinous of criminals like rapists, murderers, and oath-breakers are sentenced to suffer in Nastrond.

The Structure of Society

Every religion in this world strives to establish a structure in society. This is one of the main functions of a religion, to maintain law and order by restructuring so-called past barbaric traditions. And, Asatru also divides society into a well-defined structure with different subgroups. These divisions aren't as rigid or exploitative as in the other religions, but they provide a solid foundation on which to build society.

The Asatruars are divided into smaller groups called "kindred," which are local groups often made up of an extended family. The kindred have also been called Garth/Stead/Skeppslag. This group is not affiliated with any nation but is composed of people who are related by blood or marriage, and as a subdivision, is small enough to be well connected, but large enough to be influential in itself.

The leader of a kindred is known as Gothar, and they're responsible for the priestly functions. The word Gothar means someone who speaks the tongue of gods. The responsibilities of a Gothar have varied throughout the centuries, and sometimes they were put in charge of establishing temples.

Most Important Gods and Goddesses

The Norse deities that Asatruar worship has recently become better known. Movies, comics, and TV shows have adapted various interesting gods and goddesses into mainstream pop culture. Most people are aware of the thunder god Thor, the trickster god Loki, the all-father Odin, and even the Valkyries.

Odin is the supposed leader of the Aesir gods and was also worshipped as a god of war. However, his role wasn't limited to being the god of a single aspect. Odin has been associated with various fields, and he was even considered the god of poets. The one-eyed god was also called Woden/Wotan/Wodan in various records which have been unearthed. Odin's importance can be understood by tracing the source of the word "Wednesday" as it is derived from "Woden's Day." The one-eyed Odin was considered a wise man, well-versed in magic and it is said he gained all his knowledge by hanging himself on the Yggdrasil tree for nine nights, giving up his eye in the process. Odin also married the goddess Freyja and fathered many children, including Thor.

Freyja, also known as Friggs or Frey, is the goddess of fertility and sexuality. For this reason, she was very popular among women in ancient times. Freyja was Odin's wife, and she was the one who escorted all the fallen heroes to Valhalla along with her Valkyries. She's considered the goddess of beauty and love due to her relationship with fertility and sex. The Asatru gods are all assigned multiple roles, and they aren't limited in scope. The same can be seen in the case of Freyja, who was also worshipped as a goddess of the household because one of her roles was to protect married women.

Thor is the single most well-known Norse god due to the various comics and movies in which he features. He's portrayed as the god of storms, which is why he was also worshipped by many in later eras when the Vikings' focus shifted to farming rather than war. Thor is depicted as an embodiment of masculine energy, and just like his mother Freyja, he is also associated with fertility. This is due to his ravenous sexual appetite and similar sexual escapades to the Greek god of thunder Zeus. Thor wields a war hammer, Mjölnir, and he was called by the other gods whenever a beast or a giant threatened the peace established by Aesir.

Another very popular god of the Norse pantheon was Loki. Despite being an Aesir, Loki was devious and was considered a trickster god. Contrary to the popular depictions of Loki, he's not the brother of Thor or adopted son of Odin. Loki is considered to be similar to Odin in terms of stature and has also been depicted as Odin's brother in many places. He, along with the above-mentioned 3 major gods, was a major deity. It's even predicted that during Ragnarök-the Norse apocalypse, Loki would shift his allegiances and fight alongside the Jotnar to kill Odin. However, Loki wasn't an evil god by any means. He was a balancing power who questioned everything and expanded

CHAPTER 4

GODS AND GODDESSES

the boundaries of a society in which order was maintained by Odin and the others.

Odin

S on of the giant Borr and Bestla, the daughter of Bolþọrn, Odin is the oldest of the Æsir. Born in ancient times, he and his brothers, Vili and Vé, were the creators of creation. They killed the primitive giant Ymir and, with his carcass, forged the earth and the sky. Then they regulated the course of the stars, established the computation of time, and founded the new universal order.

Odin is supreme among the gods and governs all things in the world. Although the other gods are also powerful, everyone serves him, as children do with their father. In fact, he is called Allfọðr, "father of all," because he is the father of the gods and of men, the creator of all that he has brought to completion with his power.

Odin resides in Asgard, in the silver palace called Valaskjálf, "fortress of the elect," which he himself raised. In that room is the throne Hliðskjálf, from which Odin observes the whole world and the conduct of every man, and understands all the things he sees.

Hella

Hella is the daughter of Loki and the giantess, Angrboda. She is often depicted as half a beautiful maiden and half a corpse.

Hella is most notably known for being the ruler of the underworld, and all those who pass due to old age, sickness, or natural causes are meant to enter her halls. Hella was given this position by Odin who somewhat exiled her to the realm of the dead due to her 'unsightly' appearance.

She is associated with crows and a hellhound named Garmr.

Bragi

Among the Æsirs there is a god called Bragi. He is the son of Odin and possesses vast wisdom. Runes are carved on his tongue, and perhaps this is why he is so eloquent in speaking. He is even more skilled in the art of poetry, of which he is said to be the creator. From its name stems the skaldic art called bragr; a man or woman who possesses, to the maximum degree, dominion over the word is called a bragi. Equipped with a long and thick beard, he knows all the kenningars and poetic metaphors by heart, and explained them to Irgir during a banquet, without hiding from him the myths and stories from which they had originated.

Bragi's wife is Iðunn, the Goddess who guards the apples of youth. Bragi has children and also adopted children.

He is certainly not a warrior. Bragi, although he appears proud when necessary and claims to be ready to fight with anyone, prefers to calm tempers rather than exacerbate them. When Loki insulted him, at Irgir's court, calling him a coward, he preferred to quiet the situation by giving him a horse, a sword, and a bracelet. But since the other did not cease provoking him, Bragi declared, in no uncertain terms, that he would have cut off his head if they had not been guests in the hall of the marine giant.

On the other hand, despite not being a fighter, Bragi attends Valhalla, where, together with Hermóðr, he welcomes the renowned sovereigns who fall in battle.

Thor

Thor is another Norse god that has captured the imagination of modern society and media. He has been represented in numerous media and art forms, most notably the Marvel comics and cinematic universe where he is portrayed as an Avenger.

Thor is the god of thunder and uses his hammer, Mjölnir, to control lightning and thunder. Strangely enough, Mjölnir is also considered a symbol of fertility.

He is also known as a patron of those who work the land, such as farmers and agricultural workers.

Contrary to popular belief, Thor is not a son of Odin and instead was fathered by Jord. He is also known as the 'son of Earth' (*Asatru Deities—The Standing Stone Society*, n.d.), and therefore, Thor is also closely affiliated to Earth.

Much like Odin, Thor is also revered as a warrior god, and in some texts, is thought of as the protector of Asgard.

Loki

Loki is a central figure in the development of many Norse myths. The shrewd god of cunning and chaos, an ingenious master of deception, skilled in double speech, more than a divine figure, he is the personification of fraudulent cunning and the subtle art of deception.

Loki is not referred to as an evil god in an absolute sense. He alternately helps gods and giants according to whose line of action is most pleasant and advantageous for him at that time. He knows and embraces the principle of the male, inflicting Asgard with his lies, but defends and preserves the principle of good to maintain the balance of opposites until the end of time. His presence is, then, fundamental because this man must necessarily oppose the good.

Loki has physical traits of exceptional beauty, which, at the same time, inspire admiration and fear, a sign of the ambiguity that characterizes him. He is the son of the giants Farbauti, "cruel attack," and Laufey, "leafy island," but he made a pact of alliance with Odin, playing on the roots of the giant blood of the Father of the Gods, being included among the Æsir.

Being of uncertain sexual boundaries, he is famous for having given birth to a progeny of ruthless beings, evil instruments whose only purpose is destruction and death. However, he also generated Sleipnir, Odin's trusty and fast horse.

He is the father of Angrbodha, the giant prostitute who was condemned to the stake for her crimes. When her body was reduced to ashes, Loki, entranced by the spectacle of death he had witnessed, took his daughter's heart, which mysteriously survived the flames, and devoured it. The evil heart, fruit of his own blood, fertilized its father, who later gave birth to three monstrous creatures: a wolf, a great snake, and a girl. All three were raised in Jotunheim until Odin discovered the deception. Presuming their danger, the father of the gods ordered them to be brought before him so that he could decide how to neutralize them. The progeny of Loki would prove to be as evil as, if not more than, their father.

Idunna

Idunna is the wife of Bragi and is described as being quite naive and simple. She is best known as the keeper of the golden apples, which keep the gods youthful and strong.

It is believed that the golden apples are completely useless unless given by Idunna's own hand. Therefore, the regenerative power of the apples stems from Idunna herself.

Idunna is thus the goddess of growth and vegetation and her symbols are an apple and seeds. She can also be interpreted as being a goddess of routine since the gods are compelled to visit her orchard daily in order to receive their apple.

Tyr

Tyr was the first Sky-god/Sky-father and head of the pantheon, who would later be overthrown by Odin. He was also known as Saxnot and is believed to be the ancient ancestor of the kings of Essex.

Tyr is the patron god of judges and lawyers, and those who speak for justice and enforce order. Thus, he is often evoked in times of legal disputes, in times of justice, order, or arbitration.

Interestingly enough, even though Tyr is the god of justice and truth, he swore a false oath in order to bind the wolf Fenris. However, he would pay for this oath with his right hand.

As the myth goes, Tyr placed his hand inside Fenris' mouth as a sign of good faith; however, once Fenris discovered he'd been deceived, he bit off the hand.

This myth greatly shifted the perceptions of Tyr and showed him to respect not only laws and justice, but that he also has the courage to break these laws for the good of the people. Thus, Tyr represents both order and justice and allows us to question what justice really is.

Heimdall

Heimdall is the keeper of Asgard and Bifrost, the rainbow bridge that connects heaven and earth, Asgard with Midgard, which men can admire only after storms. His sister is Sif, the wife of Thor.

The reason for the relationship with Sif is not very clear. It is said that, in fact, Heimdallr was the son of nine different mothers and not of one, while his father was Odin, in turn, Thor's father.

It is said of Heimdallr that he is a shining god of light and that he is also a valiant soldier and an expert warrior.

He watches tirelessly and, like Odin, has received great power by depriving himself of a part of his body: He cut and buried one of his ears under Yggdrasil, receiving, in exchange, very fine sight and hearing. Heimdall is capable of sensing every threat in the universe.

He is the owner of the Gjallarhorn magic horn, with which he can call and warn the gods in the event of an attack. During Ragnarök, this horn will resound, grave and penetrating, in all nine worlds, calling to the final clash the forces of good against those of evil. Heimdall will witness the collapse of Bifrost, shattered by the destroyers of the universe, and will fight against Loki. He will succeed in killing Loki and will still play his horn for a last, short time before dying from the wounds he has sustained, with the image of the end of the universe imprinted in his eyes.

Two creatures that accompany Heimdallr are the golden cock Gullinkamb, which has the task of waking Odin's soldiers every morning to incite them to battle, and the golden horse Gultopp.

Vidarr

Vidar, the second strongest Æsir after Thor, is the son of Odin and the giantess Gríðr. He lives in Asgard in the peaceful hall Vidi, with a great garden. He is known for being silent and at peace with nature in his garden, working on a special shoe.

This shoe is the strongest existing shoe and is made from all the scraps and pieces of leather trashed in Midgard.

Baldur

Baldur is the son of Odin and Frigga. Strangely enough, unlike most Aesir gods, Baldur is known for his death rather than his life.

The myth states that Baldur was the most beloved of all the gods and was generally held in high regard. However, after he began experiencing a series of nightmares, his mother, Frigga, consulted the oracles who prophesied his death.

In order to avoid this fate, Frigga gained a promise from each living thing, except the mistletoe, which she deemed weak, that they wouldn't cause Baldur harm. With the surety that nothing living would harm Baldur, the gods decided to make a game out of throwing things at him and watching them bounce harmfully off his body.

However, Loki, god of mischief, saw this as an opportunity. Loki gave Hodur, Baldur's brother, a dart made of mistletoe so that he could join in with the game. Baldur was pierced by the dart and died immediately.

Baldur and his wife Nanna thus reside in the realm of the dead and are saved from Ragnarok.

Freyja

Freyja is the Goddess of love but is also associated with lust, fertility, sex, and war. She lives on Fólkvangr, the "camp of the people" and is the daughter of Njord. She has a twin, Freyr, and is married to the god Odr. With him, she has two children: Hnoss and Gersemi.

Despite being a Vanir, she became an honorable member of the Æsir after the end of the war between the Æsir and Vanir.

She is said to have a beautiful appearance and long golden hair and is often represented as having a wild, sylvan appearance, wearing a dress made of flowers (or sometimes a green dress), and surrounded by animals. She is desired not just among the gods and goddesses but also among giants and dwarves. She loves jewelry and fine materials and has quite often used her beauty to get what she desires. She owns the necklace known as Brísingamen.

Freyja loves to travel with her chariot, pulled by two cats. She is also able to fly with her cloak of falcon feathers. Freyja has a boar named Hildisvíni, which she rides when she is not using her chariot.

Her marriage to Odr is said to be very happy, although he is often absent from home, leaving his bride in tears made of gold.

It is not certain, however, if Freyja is faithful to him, as the other gods—especially Loki—often accused her of being lustful.

Forseti

Forseti, the son of Nanna and Baldr, is the law-speaker and the god of justice. Most of the time, he is the judge who decides the outcome of a dispute between the gods. He applies the fairest judgment. Sometimes he spends his day in the practice of meditation.

Freyr

Freyr, one of the most beautiful gods, is the god of fertility, prosperity, wealth, and harvest. Member of the Vanir, he is the son of Njord. Freyr has a twin sister named Freyja and is married to the giantess Gerðr. On the day of Ragnarök, Freyr will pay for this love with his life.

Often, he uses his chariot, conveyed by his boar, named Gullinbursti, to travel long distances.

Frigg

She is the queen of Asgard and the wife of Odin. They have two sons: Baldr and Hodr. She is the stepmother of Bragi, Heimdall, Hermod, Höder, Tyr, Vidar, Thor, and Vali.

The origin of another symbol of hers—namely, the bunch of keys—is not known. It was said that Frigg always kept a bunch of keys but the myth that explains the reason for this has been lost over time. One explanation is that the keys represent the goddess's ability to open the doors of unknown worlds, increasing her knowledge or ability to see the future.

She is the only one permitted to sit on Odin's high seat, "Hlidskjalf," and look out over the universe.

Her three handmaids are Fulla, Gná, and Hlín. The first, always next to the mistress, has the task of serving her and assisting her inside the domestic walls, and, in particular, in the Fensalir, Frigg's personal home within Asgard. Hlín has the task of acting as an ambassador and carrying messages from the goddess to the earth under the guise of a hawk. Gná fulfills some of Fulla's duties and some of Hlín's duties.

Fulla is the most important of the three. She is depicted with long hair, always at Frigg's feet, very often holding a casket, as it was believed that one of her most important tasks is to carefully fold her mistress's stockings or shoes. Winter was sacred to Frigg and Fulla, especially the days immediately after the solstice, during which the girls are forbidden to spin as a sign of respect to the queen of the gods. Fulla, in addition to being a maid, is also Frigg's confidante and keeper of her secrets.

The ability of the maiden Hlín to transform herself into a hawk derives from a cloak woven with hawk feathers—perhaps by Frigg herself. This cloak has the property of making anyone who wears it capable of flying.

Njord

Njord is the god of the wind. He is a Vanir and is the father of Freyja and Freyr. Njord is married to the giantess Skadi.

Mimir

Mimir is the god of knowledge and wisdom. During the war between the Asir and Vanir, Mimir was sent to the Vanir. However, the Vanir beheaded Mimir and sent his head back to Asgard. Odin, to retain Mimir's wisdom, preserved his head with magic so that he can provide his knowledge.

Frigga

Frigga, also known as Frigg, is the wife of Odin and is known to be very wise. She is believed to be the patron of married women and mothers. Frigga is the goddess of childbirth, small children, and mothers, as well as the hearth.

CHAPTER 5

TOASTS, BOASTS, AND OATHS

Frigga is often likened to Freya of the Vanir, and over time, their myths and roles have melded together. In fact, it is quite difficult to untangle them, and for all intents and purposes, they are one and the same (*Freya and Frigg–Norse Mythology and Religion*, n.d.).

With this fusion of Frigga and Freya, Frigga gained powerful magical abilities, which were said to rival that of Odin. In fact, Frigga taught Odin much of what he knew.

Frigga is often represented by a spinning wheel, mistletoe, and silver.

It is the way a practitioner views the world, it is the way they decide to practice Asatru, and it is the way they behave and treat others.

The heathen perspective of creation and time is heavily based on the myth of creation and Norse mythology, which has been discussed in Chapters 1 and 3. Therefore, I won't be wasting your precious time by rehashing them.

Heathenry, much like other beliefs and religions, has its own ethical and moral code. In Asatru, this code is known as the Nine Noble Virtues (NNV). The NNV stems from Edred Thorsson or Stephen McNallen, depending on which texts you read (accounts vary). It is known as a 'distillation' of the basic virtues and themes that have been interpreted from the myths and legends of the Viking age.

While these virtues are important within general society, something that I've noticed is that they are not nearly as weighted or emphasized. While they are recognized as valuable, it wouldn't matter much if one or more were absent.

For example, industriousness is valued; however, if a person decided not to employ this virtue, societal opinion of them wouldn't change much. Their lack of industriousness would affect them more than anything else.

My point here is that while general society views these virtues as important, society doesn't really perceive them as being vital.

Oaths

In the perspective of Asatru, an oath is a promise. It is a guarantee. Upholding an oath is more than just remaining truthful, it is a display of honor and integrity.

In Asatru, an oath holds the weight of a vow.

In my experience, because of the weight that oaths hold, you should not easily make them, nor should they be easily broken.

In general society, honesty and integrity are quite important. They instill trust and strengthen friendships, and while it is important to stick to your promises, they don't hold the same weight as an oath.

For the most part, and with few exceptions, promises can be broken without many lasting consequences. Your friends and family might be upset with you for a bit, but it generally isn't anything an apology can't fix.

With oaths, it is completely different. Breaking an oath means dishonoring yourself and could tarnish your reputation within the community.

Worship

The heathen perspective of worship is quite complicated. There isn't one single way to worship the gods of your ancestors. There is no right way to worship the gods. It all depends on you and how you choose to practice and worship.

Ancestor veneration is also a common worship practice. Ancestors are quite an important part of Asatru, and it is believed that the dead remain in our lives and often confer blessings on the community and their loved ones.

Therefore, they are revered by their descendants.

Asatru practitioners are also able to practice worship by living their lives according to the NNV and by honoring the gods through their lifestyles.

The key point here is that, as Asatru practitioners, we have the freedom to worship as we wish, as long as it is done respectfully and with dignity.

The perspective of worship within general society is as varied and open-ended as it is in Asatru. Practices of worship differ and are heavily dependent on the culture and religion of the area. The worship practices within Hinduism are very different from Christianity.

A major difference between Asatru worship and other religions is the presence of a prescribed dogma and scripture, such as the Bible or the Torah. Most religions have strict practices and methods of worship that are shared across communities,

CHAPTER 6

Magic and Esoteric Practices, What You Need and How to Perform Them

regions, and countries.

While the methods and practices differ, I would argue that the perspective of worship is the same. Both Asatru and Abrahamic religions worship as a means to thank their god or gods and honor these deities.

Magic is often a label that is stuck on the Norse, the Vikings, and pagans in general, but the word 'pagan' really only means "someone who doesn't believe in the most popular god or gods of the time." This is a simplistic breakdown of it, but when you boil it down this is what it means. Maybe this is why it scares people, but the general population has always been afraid of what they can't or don't want to understand.

Anything strange or 'supernatural' will always be viewed as magic, and the ones who shout the loudest that it doesn't exist would be the first to just label that very phenomenon as science if it was suddenly proven. This is why we must always keep an open mind when we think about magic as a whole, as if you genuinely believe in it, then the first, and most important, step has been made.

Magic Rituals and Spells

Spells and magic are the ability to influence the things around us, not to control or physically change them. This is extremely important to remember. Much like how a strong personality in a boardroom can influence the proceedings, when we practice these things we are helping to direct the energies that we want in a more positive direction. Using our magic, or 'magick,' for our own benefit is perfectly fine, but if you go into this believing that you will be able to instantly alter your life, then you will be disappointed.

You will see positive changes from the beginning, that is for certain, but they will be intricate and quiet for the most part. Spells are something personal, and they are designed to help us to improve ourselves. Casting a spell in the morning to help start your day can be as easy as taking a few moments to center yourself and envisioning a particular rune, or even just holding it for a while and repeating a few words as to what you want help with. Something as simple as saying a prayer to one of the Nordic gods before you leave the house can be sufficient.

All of these actions and more are spells. They are some of the more basic spells, sure, but they work for the beginner in amazing ways. As you become more and more comfortable, you can then move on to more powerful and elaborate spells and rituals, but charging a talisman and embracing its energy or partaking in a regular ritual will do more for you than one huge gesture every few months. This is about maintaining a spiritual journey, and once you keep practicing regularly, then the intensity and details of what you practice will grow naturally.

Remember that belief in what you are doing here is a spell. Saying a prayer to Odin and asking for guidance is a spell. Consecrating a talisman is a spell. Along with these small efforts, you will have your rituals as a starting point, which are also spells in their own right. Your divination will come from your reading of the runes, and with all of the layouts and energies that we have discussed together, you will be on the way to pure enlightenment before you know it.

Remember that all of the rituals and spells performed by the Norse, and the Vikings later on, were never written down. The records we have are from outsiders who either didn't understand what they were seeing and just blindly wrote down what they couldn't fathom, or even worse, were only transcribing second or third hand accounts of how it works.

In showing you the rituals themselves, I will give you the basic three that are more designed to start you off and set you up for later, more powerful experiences. Do not feel downhearted, as with your casting and knowledge of the Elder Futhark, you are only here to begin your journey, and once you have packed sufficiently, then the destination is up to you. The Norse would have only had this to work with too. How they came to be as foresighted and enlightened as they were came through time and unwavering belief in their ability to see.

Ritual of Protection and Peace of Mind

First off, you will need two runes and a stick, pointer, staff, or wand. Usually, Hagalaz and Elhaz are preferred here, and I recommend that these be your choice as well. If you decide to do this ritual indoors, as many do, you will need to draw an imaginary circle around you when you begin, unless you don't mind getting chalk all over your floor! Of course, if you are doing it outside, then this will not be a problem, so go to town.

Draw your imaginary or physical line at arm's length all the way around. You do not have to do it perfectly, as the most important thing is that it is a complete circle. Once this is done, stand in the center and face in a northerly direction. This is always a good practice in any Norse ritual or spell.

Now you must close your eyes and envision Fehu. Call its image to the forefront of your thoughts and hold it there. Once this is done, try and bring the image down before you so it is centered between the tip of your head and your toes. Take one sidestep clockwise and release the image into the universe, and after this, you will need to do the same with the rest of the Elder Futhark, moving on to Uraz next, before finally getting to Othala, and then Fehu again, and thus completing the circle. Remember to visualize each one before centering it, using the visual explanations provided earlier, or whatever way suits you best.

Next, form a cross with your body, having your arms out parallel to the ground and your back straight, being sure to be facing north again. Close your eyes and visualize the outer rim of your circle. Once this is done, call up an image of another cross facing you, this should be of equal size to the one you are forming, so the two centers are directly across. Hold this pose and image until you feel a little more relaxed. It will come, so don't stress.

Choose a third rune in your mind. This should be relevant to how you want to proceed, be it an issue you face or a strength you want to be improved. Now that you have the image before you, draw it in the air with your staff or wand, really concentrating on shaping it correctly. This will do two things:

it will please the gods and it will focus your mind.

Now that you have found your rhythm, recite this incantation, "(your chosen rune) *I Nordhri helga ve theta ok hald vorgh.*" This translates as, "(your chosen rune) in the North hallow and hold this holy stead." These are the words of protection that our ancestors recited each day, and when we use them today, they bring the same peace of mind into our lives.

Here, you can choose another rune, again being sure to pick one that means something to you or the situation, and after making your choice, you can then turn the east, and say, "(your chosen rune) *I Austri helga ve theta ok hald viirdh.*" This, of course, means the same, only with your chosen rune and north replaced by east. Do not take this explanation to be dismissive in any way, I am only breaking it down for you without any unnecessary nonsense.

Next, you will turn to the south and add your newly envisioned rune to the beginning of the incantation, followed by, "... *I Sudhri helga ve theta ok hald viirdh.*"

Turning west, you will choose your final rune and bring its image to the forefront of your thoughts, and again draw the image with your staff while repeating, "(chosen rune) *I Vestri helga ve thetta ok hald viirdh.*" (Thorsson, 2020)

Returning to the north, you may now begin to wind down. This will involve calling up the images of your two originally chosen runes, and of course, the four that followed as you recited the word of our forefathers in the four hallowed corners. Once you have these symbols before you, bring them down once more to your core and let them fade to where they may. Be sure to relax your mind and body.

Once you are done, take some time to yourself to take it all in on a subconscious level. I would suggest only practicing this ritual for a while before moving on to the other that we will cover shortly. This is only to lower the risk of becoming overwhelmed or disheartened.

Talisman

Something that we will always associate with magic is a talisman, and this is the easiest and best example to use when discussing spells. The beauty of a talisman is that it can be anything that you desire, which makes it personal to you. The energies that you attach to it are also your choice, so take your time when making this decision and try to remember that there is only so much energy in the universe, so do not get into the habit of creating an endless array of charms.

A talisman is any object that you empower with your fate, energy, or spirit. This will involve first cleansing the object, charging it, and consecrating it. How you do this will be entirely up to you, as only you will know what energies and positivity you will want from the object, but much like choosing which rune you believe will give you answers, this will come to you internally, so keep your mind open.

Once you have made your choice, you can draw an imaginary circle as you did before. If you have one permanently drawn somewhere, then of course that is fantastic. Hold the rune at your center and close your eyes. Envision the symbol of what you have chosen and bring it before your mind's eye. Keeping it there for a couple of minutes will help release any tension and open up your being to more positive energy.

Before you let go of the image, repeat a pre-memorized prayer that you have created in your own words, or if you haven't done this, then just ask for the guidance that you seek. These words that you create on the spot are the essence of all prayers anyhow, so whatever you say, no matter how silly you may unnecessarily feel, will be the exact words that you need to say.

You will know instinctively when you are ready to finish casting the spell, as the energy around you will shift. This will

CHAPTER 7

Heathen Rituals, What You Need and How to Perform Them

not happen with the room shaking or an object moving, but there will be a feeling that you will know when it occurs. The reason that I cannot really explain the exact nature of it here is that it not only varies from person to person, but it can change according to each spell too. Just enjoy it when it comes, and let the spell that you have cast work its way into the universe.

Finishing the spell is only a matter of stepping out of the circle and placing the rune you had chosen back into the pouch. If you feel the need to hold your hand in for an extra few minutes to absorb all that they have to give, then go ahead. It will not interfere with the spell that you have just cast in any way.

Heathenry is a new religious movement that is known by multiple other terms, including Heathenism, Germanic Neopaganism, or contemporary Germanic Paganism. It was developed in Europe in the early 20th century and is based on pre-Christian beliefs followed by the Germanic tribes from the Iron Age until the Early Middle Ages.

Heathenry is an attempt to revive and reconstruct ancient belief systems using remaining evidence from folklore, history, and archeology. Heathenry is a polytheistic belief system that focuses on a pantheon of gods, goddesses, and deities from the pre-Christian era of the Germanic regions. The followers of this new religious movement have adopted the cosmological perspectives from ancient societies and tribes. They believe in animism too, or that the cosmos, including the natural world we see around us, are filled with spirits and other divine beings and creatures.

"Heathens," as the followers of Heathenry call themselves, believe in a system of ethics based on loyalty, personal integrity, and honor. Beliefs in the afterlife are varied, but this topic does not get much attention among the Heathens.

Practitioners are trying to understand and revive forgotten belief systems by using one or more of the following sources:

- Old Norse texts related to Iceland, including the *Poetic Edda* and *Prose Edda*.
- Old English recordings such as Beowulf.
- German texts of the Middle Ages such as *Nibelungenlied*.
- Archeological evidence that throws light on the pre-Christian age of northern Europe.
- Folklore-based stories and tales collectively referred to as "Lore" by Heathens.

Heathenry believers perform sacrificial rites and rituals referred to as "blots," where a variety of libations and food are offered to their deities. Most of the rituals include a ceremony called symbel, which consists of offering a toast of an alcoholic beverage to the gods. Some practitioners also perform rituals to achieve an altered state of reality through visions and wisdom from the invisible spiritual beings and deities. The most popular of these rituals include the seiðr and galdr.

While some practitioners indulge in these rituals individually, some Heathens perform the ceremonies in little groups called "kindreds" or "hearths." The group rituals are usually conducted in open spaces or in buildings constructed specifically for this purpose.

Heathenry predates Christianity and other Abrahamic faiths. It is believed to have been originally practiced by Northern European people who lived over a thousand years ago. These people were the Anglo-Saxon English, Scandinavians, and Germans.

While these faiths faced harsh persecution under Christian expansion, their modern-day revival has seen very little opposition. Modern heathenistic groups include Asatru and Germanic Pagan Reconstructionism.

Simply put, heathenistic faith is not an organized religion. There exists no one dogma or means of practicing the faith. Each group or individual has the freedom to develop their own practices and beliefs.

Heathen Rituals

The Blot

The blot is a Heathenry ritual where offerings are given to the gods. Exchanging gifts was an important aspect of early Germanic tribes and societies. Giving gifts was a way of making and maintaining friendships and relationships. Gift exchanges among family and kinsfolk were a way of bonding with each other and reflecting the responsibility of each member toward the community as a whole. Interestingly, the offering of gifts to gods and goddesses had the same connotation.

In a blot ceremony, the priests and/or priestesses invoke the gods and seek their help. They then use a branch or sprig of an evergreen tree to sprinkle mead on the idols of the deities. The offering is also sprinkled on the assembled participants. The ritual could be improvised as it progresses, or the priests and priestesses could follow a strict structure and script. There are no hard and fast rules for it.

When the sprinkling is done, and the gods invoked, the bowl of mead is emptied into the fire or the earth, signifying the final libation. Often, the blot ritual is followed by a communal meal, which forms part of the ritual itself.

When your preparations are done, you can begin the 9-step blot ritual process as follows:

Vigia—The Dedication: A blot begins with a dedication of the altar and the ritual's sacred space to the gods or vigia. The officiating priest or priestess sends up prayers of dedication to the gods in the form of songs or hallowed verses, while the other participants use various responses at the end of each hallowed verse. Here is a simple example of a hallowed verse you can use in the dedication step: "We call upon all the deities and ancestors to come and dwell in this hallowed space."

Helgia—The Consecration: In the consecration process, the sacred fire purifies the air of the sacred space where the ritual is taking place. The need-fire is carried around the perimeter of the ritual space as a hallowed verse is chanted by the participants and/or the officiating priest or priestess.

Bidja—The Prayer: The bidja is the holy prayer of the blot ritual. It is usually performed with the rune Elgr or Elhaz. The participants stand erect and raise their arms over their heads in a "Y" formation as they focus on the idols of the deities on the altar. This segment is about connecting with the deities and gods of the ritual within the perimeter of the sanctified area.

Blota (Also Called Offra)—The Offering: This step concerns the offering to the gods, which is the central part of the blot ritual. Different offerings are given to different gods depending on the needs and time of the year. While animal sacrifices were part of the ritual in ancient times, in modern days, mead is the most common and popular offering. Odin is believed to live and survive on honey mead only, and therefore, it is considered an ideal offering to the gods in any ritual.

Senda—The Sending: Now, it is time to send the offerings to the gods. There are many ways to do so, and all of them use the four elements, including fire, water, earth, and air, to send the offerings. In ancient times (thanks to archeological evidence), we know that plates of offerings were submerged in water, buried under the earth, left hanging from a tree, or put into the sacrificial fire.

Signa—The Blessing: According to Norse gift exchange traditions, it is now time to receive our gifts from the gods in return for our gifts to them. The officiating priest or priestess dips the evergreen sprig into the mead in the offering bowl and sprinkles it on all of the assembled people. An example of a hallowed verse for this occasion is given below: "Hail to you, almighty gods and goddesses, We solemnly thank you for your blessings."

Kjosa—The Choosing: This step is about interpreting the message of the gods. In a blot ritual, the lot box or peord filled with runes is first offered to the gods seeking their message.

"We offer these runes to you, mighty gods, We seek your message for us, powerful gods, Tell us what we need to know, And bless us with your wisdom."

Then, each of the participants picks up one rune from the lot box. The interpretations of the rune they pick are then used as guidance points in their coming days.

Soa—The Consuming: Sumbel is a drinking ritual that is often performed to consume the consecrated mead. The sumbel is described in detail in the next section of this chapter.

Enda—The Closing: This entire blot ritual is now in the concluding stage. The officiating person performs a closing ceremony allowing everyone to return to their mundane, routine world after their communion with the world of gods and goddesses, leaving the participants empowered and strengthened. This step involves hailing and thanking the gods for spending time with the participants and seeking their permission to close the blot ceremony.

"Hail to the gods who heard us, Hail to the goddesses who heard us, We thank you from the bottom of our hearts, Watch over us and our world."

Sumbel

Sumbel is another common drinking ritual followed by practicing Heathens. Also spelled as symbel, this is a ritual drinking ceremony in which the practitioners raise a toast to their gods. Often, a sumbel follows a blot ritual and involves a drinking horn in which the consecrated and blessed mead is filled. The drinking horn is passed among the assembled practitioners three times, signifying the past, present, and future.

Odinshorn signifies our past, Thorshorn our present, and Freyshorn, our future. Some of the practitioners sip directly from the drinking horn or pour a little of the drink into their own glasses, and as each person does so, he or she makes a comment or a toast to the gods, according to his or her needs.

During the sumbel ceremony, toasts are made to the gods, goddesses, and deities. Verbal tributes are also made to the ancestors, gods, and heroes from Norse mythology. After this, oaths are taken with regard to future actions. Oaths and promises made during such ceremonies are considered binding for the oath-takers, thanks to the high level of sacredness rendered to this ceremony.

In a sumbel ceremony, the toasts made to the gods and the tributes paid to the ancestors help the worshippers connect with and harness their powers and use them in their own lives. In modern times, sumbel has a powerful social role to play in Heathenry. It is a place and time when bonds are cemented, political moves are made, peace is negotiated, and newfound relationships and partnerships are forged in the Heathen community.

Sumbel ceremonies are conducted with a focus on children, too, for which the drinking horn is filled with apple juice instead of mead. During the toast paying tributes to the gods, children tape pictures of apples onto a poster of a tree, which symbolizes the apple tree of Goddess Idunn.

At this point, it might make sense to summarize the differences between sumbel and blot in Asatru. A blot is a ceremonial prayer that can range from a simple individual ritual wherein only the practitioner lifts a mug of coffee or drink to share with the gods, to a large community event that happens on a football field. The small blot can be done individually at home regularly, while formalized Heathenism organizations handle the bigger ones.

Sumbel, on the other hand, is like a sacred drinking party where gods are toasted, and the participants sing their tributes even as the drinking horn is passed around. Each person takes oaths and boasts as the drinking horn is passed around. A group blot is an awe-inspiring experience, while a sumbel is a great bonding experience for practitioners.

Seidr and Galdr

Seidr is a religious practice in Heathenism that consists of a shamanic ritual trance. Scholars tend to believe that modern seidr practices could have been developed during the 1990s when Neo-Shamanism was developed and popularized, though older forms of seidr are described in many sagas. One of the most popular seidr practices of the ancient followers of Norse Paganism is referred to as oracular or high-seat seidr, which is described in Eiriks saga or the Saga of Erik the Red. This saga is an account of the exploration of North America by the Nordic people.

In the oracular seidr ritual, a seidr practitioner sits on a high seat. Chants and songs are used to invoke the gods and wights. Drumming, a popular element in Shamanism, is used to induce an altered state of consciousness in the practitioner. In this altered state of consciousness, the practitioner undertakes a meditative journey where they travel through the World Tree to Helheim.

The assembled participants ask questions to which they need answers. The practitioner finds these answers from Helheim by speaking to the ancestor spirits, and the divine beings that reside there pass the messages and answers on to the seekers. Some seidr practitioners use entheogenic substances to achieve an altered state of consciousness.

Glade is another Asatru practice that involves singing and chanting rune names and rune poems. Runic alphabets were used to write Germanic languages before the Christian influence. Chanting and reciting these poems rhythmically in a community helps participants get into altered states of consciousness, which, in turn, helps them to seek out deities and communicate with them. Although these poems were written in a Christian context, most practitioners believe that the themes reflected in them are of a pre-Christian era. Moreover, some poems are re-appropriated for modern Heathenism.

In addition to the various blot rituals, different groups of Heathens celebrate different festivals based on their belief systems and cultures. The most common Heathen festivals celebrated by most groups include:

Winter Nights—Also known as vetrnaetr in the Old Norse language, Winter Nights refers to a three-day festival that marks the start of winter. Specific sacrifices and rituals are held during Winter Nights.

In the olden days, the King of Sweden performed a public sacrifice as part of a community event called disablot. Contrarily, alfablot was a ritual and/or sacrifice of the ancient times carried out in each household privately for specific local spirits and family deities.

Yule—Yule or Yuletide is connected to Odin, but the Christianization of this festival has resulted in Christmastide. Many customs and traditions practiced during Christmas today, including Yule goat, Yule log, and Yule singing, are

CHAPTER 8

BEING ASATRU TODAY

borrowed from Norse Pagan cultures, or so it is believed. The above festivals find mention in Heimskringla and therefore, are believed to be of ancient origins.

Rituals and rites were an integral part of ancient Norse Paganism and adorn the modern version of Asatru. Sacred and hallowed verses, beautifully crafted ritual tools, food and drink, a deep sense of bonding and connection with other believers and the gods and goddesses, etc., drive present-day Asatruars to keep the tradition of rituals and ceremonies alive.

So, what does it mean to be a modern-day heathen? How does this faith impact your lifestyle? What are the benefits? And how are modern-day heathens perceived by the public?

These questions are all quite heavy-handed and difficult to answer.

Let's look at the first one, what does it mean to be a modern-day heathen?

Well, what do you want it to mean? What it means depends entirely on you and what you want the faith to bring to your life.

So, rather than wondering what it means to be a heathen, think about what you want it to mean. The faith of Asatru doesn't force a particular lifestyle or belief on its practitioners. Unlike the Abrahamic faiths, it also doesn't do any missionary work, nor is there a move to convert people to the faith.

While there aren't any prescribed practices or scriptures, there exist a few key tenets within the faith.

The first is that Asatru centers on the Norse pantheon and your relationship to them. How you choose to practice and worship will depend on you. In fact, you don't need to practice every day if you don't wish to. However, the gods are at the center.

It is believed that the people around us shape who we are and we shape them. The influence we have on one another is important. It affects our beliefs and the choices we make.

Asatru takes the concept of family and community a step further by honoring our ancestors and holding them to a similar standard to the gods.

For me, being a practicing heathen colors everything in my life. Asatru has become a perspective, a lens through which I view the world. This faith affects the way I interact with my family, friends, and community.

It affects the way I carry myself through the world, how I perform at my job. Asatru truly is a way of life.

However, Asatru might not be all of this for you.

A key benefit of practicing Asatru is that it gives you the freedom to express your faith as you wish. You get to do what you feel is right. You choose which deities to honor and how to honor them.

While there are guidelines, they are all up for interpretation.

Another benefit of practicing Asatru is that, as much as the faith is focused on the gods, it is also focused on you. This can be seen in the Nine Noble Virtues, which often emphasize practicing self-care and striving to be the best version of yourself as key parts of practicing the faith.

Asatru is a faith that cares deeply for its practitioners and shows this by offering them complete freedom.

A great way of getting in touch with the Asatru faith and finding your way within it is by connecting to other practitioners and heathens.

Having a mentor or welcoming community can help you learn more about the faith and add a certain nuance to some of the more abstract concepts and tenets of Asatru. It also gives you a sense of community and helps you transition to a heathenistic lifestyle.

Surrounding yourself with a supportive community also offers you companionship, which is quite important in the faith. It makes it easier to learn and grow within your faith.

Many of the rituals that modern Norse pagans perform are the same as the ones Vikings and other Old Norse people performed. Some of these rituals involve:

- Honoring the gods
- Giving offerings
- Feasting together
- Raising a toast to one of the Gods
- Praying to the Gods

The main way of praying to the Norse gods is by focusing one's thoughts on the deity they wish to invoke or by chanting prayers around a bonfire with other members of their hearth.

Sacrifices and offerings can be made through the blót on traditional holy days. People can also honor the gods through their actions and words during the Sumble or a daily ritual.

In the Old Norse religion, most of the festivals were interwoven with village and farm life aspects. Survival was the ultimate goal, so a lot of the blót or blood sacrifices were performed according to the phases of the moon to ask for a good and fruitful harvest.

The most common sacrifices in ancient times were animal sacrifices, but human sacrifices also occurred. The latter, though, was reserved for extreme conditions, such as war or famine. During those times, prisoners were offered to the gods.

Artifacts were also often offered, as there has been archaeological evidence in fens and bogs, such as jewelry, weapons, and tools. This method is the preferred method of offering in modern Norse Pagan rituals. One thing to make sure of is that none of the objects offered would harm or pollute nature.

The Old Norse used to offer mead to the Æsir. However, as mead is not very common nowadays, most modern pagans prefer to give offerings of beer or wine. Offerings aren't meant to placate the gods but to express the adherent's devotion to them.

According to the lore, Óðinn loves poetry. A good way to get Óðinn's attention is to do it in the form of a poem. All in all, the Norse's way of praying is not at all similar to what one might have in mind.

The Spread of Modern Asatru across the World

Since Asatru originated in Scandinavia, the modern practice of the religion is also centered in Northern European countries such as Sweden, Norway, Germany, Iceland, Greenland, and some parts of Great Britain. Vikings were skilled travelers; therefore, the religion has made marks all over the European region, and many sources can be found in the form of graffiti, writings, stone carvings, grave goods, and many similar archeological records.

Due to this traveling and varying geographical location, an important thing that has happened over the years is that there is no one Asatru religion in one place. Everywhere it has been enriched with the cultural practices and traditions of the own culture in that particular geographical location. While the deities and the basic rituals tend to be the same, there are many different interpretations and reconstructions of Asatru around the world. Especially nowadays, with massive sources of information such as the internet, this religion has found a great many new interpretations and practices that relate it to the modern world.

When studying the variations of Asatru practiced today, it can be seen that every small community that practices the religion together has its own traditions and rituals. And then, each region, which is a combination of these small groups have their unique traditions and practices. One thing that is common about all these variations is that every Asatru practitioner is a polytheist who worships several different gods. They recognized the different capabilities, personalities, and distinct triumphs and weaknesses of each of them.

Context is extremely important when understanding these texts, and they are flexible enough to blend into modern-day scenarios seamlessly. A word used to mean "wife" can be easily changed to mean a long-term lover, including lovers of the same gender. Asatru does not discriminate. Therefore, the practitioners of this beautiful religion tend to accept all kinds of lives and love with open arms, without trying to add a superficial meaning to them just because their primary source materials mentioned something in a certain way.

The way ancient heathens viewed their deities is largely different from the ways other polytheistic religions view their gods. This holds true for the modern practice of Asatru as well. In the modern world beyond this riveting ancient religion, people like to categorize things into neat boxes, and the mere attempt to mix these things is often frowned upon. It is the reason people are still fighting to keep a binary gender identification or try to oppose the mixing of two races. Asatru religion is not like that, and it has always been quite progressive and beyond its time. The lines in this religion continue to blur, allowing space for more ideas, better definitions, clarifications, and analysis. The gods and goddesses in Asatru are rather humanistic and almost "real."

Norse Pagans don't pray conventionally, and there's no specific way to follow when it comes to praying.

Some prefer to hold group gatherings and make offerings to the gods, while others prefer to do the same on their own, in private.

Others plan and perform elaborate rituals, while some prefer just to talk.

Some might even borrow methods and rituals from other faiths and practices.

As the Faith is decentralized, not everyone agrees on which is the right way, but most agree that the gods are like family to them.

Most Norse adherents prefer not to pray with their gods in a conversational tone. This usually occurs outdoors, just like the Old Norse pagans used to. There are specific sites, like the Danish Hof Manheim, meant for rituals and ceremonies.

Finding Fellow Asatru Believers

Here are some suggestions and recommendations you can use to find fellow-Astruars in your local community or the area you live in.

The Asatru Folk Assembly is a global organization with branches and representatives found in many parts of the world. You can visit their website **https://www.runestone.org/** for more information. In addition to helping you in your research about Asatru and its customs and traditions, you can also go to their "Folkbuilder" page and connect with a team member. They, in turn, can help you find someone closer to where you live.

Another Asatru community with a presence on the Internet is The Troth **https://thetroth.org/**. You can register yourself there if you wish. Scout under the "Find your local troth representative," and you are likely to discover an individual or group closer to your place of residence.

Get in touch with the kindred in the cities closest to you and connect with them. Most of these people will have some idea of how to help you build your personal Heathen connection. Here are a few tips to help you get started:

- Do an Internet search with the words "Asatru/kindred/ Heathen, [your city name]" using different search engines. You are likely to get some results from such searches, including names, contact numbers, and addresses. You can begin with this basic information.
- Use social media platforms to find Asatru connections. Many kindred groups have a dedicated page on most of the popular social media platforms.
- You can set up a local meet group using one of the paid apps that connect with other believers. Although you might have to spend money, it could be worth your efforts. Still, you need to use this only if the earlier attempts don't work.
- Another way of contacting Heathens is to get in touch with other Pagan believers in your area, such as Wiccans. Considering that many Heathens start their Asatru journey from Wiccan beliefs, these connections are likely to help you get in touch with practicing Asatruars.

Temples

Manheim opened in Denmark in 2016 and was the first pagan hof in the country since the Middle Ages.

Other modern Pagan temples currently operating are the

Ásaheimur Hof, in Efri Ás, Skagafjörður, and the Arctic Henge (Heimskautsgerðið), in Raufarhöfn in Iceland. The Odinist Fellowship Temple, in Newark-On-Trent in the United Kingdom, the Baldurshof, Asatru Folk Assembly temple, in Murdock, Minnesota, the New Grange Hall Asatru Hof, in Brownsville, Yuba County, California, and the Thorshof, Asatru Folk Assembly temple, in Linden, North Carolina, in the United States.

CHAPTER 9

Modern Asatru Practices

Apart from those, there are two temples under construction, one in the United States and one in Iceland.

The first is the Atlanta Heathen Hof, which will be a temple for the group Vör Fórn Siðr. It is 10 miles outside Atlanta, Georgia, and will hopefully be fully completed by 2022.

The second one is in Reykjavik, Iceland. The Hof Ásatrúarfélagsins is under construction by the Ásatrúarfélagið and is currently being built in stages as it has been delayed several times.

Reykjavik, Iceland

Norse Paganism, rooted in ancient practices and beliefs, survives to this day, but not without adaptation to the modern world. Keep in mind that there are two ways to adapt and evolve. The first is to deviate from one's core values and sacrifice one's identity for the sake of survival. It would have been a betrayal of Norse Paganism's core beliefs and values if it had done so. The second method of adaptation is to allow the modern world in, allowing it to express the core beliefs and values in its own unique way. That is how Asatru survived and continues to survive without change. When we examine the differences between Asatru in ancient times and in the modern world, you'll be able to see that the religion itself hadn't changed one bit. However, this was not always the case.

As with any foreign concept or set of beliefs, the general public had a hard time accepting Asatru into its midst, especially given that it is based on Norse mythology. For the time being, suffice it to say that the first Asatruars had a difficult time carving out a place for themselves in the world, but they were ultimately successful in changing modern attitudes toward Norse Paganism. In this chapter, we look at the modern manifestation of Asatru: the form in which it exists, how it came to exist in that form, the modern believers, and more.

Common practices include making offerings to the gods and goddesses and perhaps prayers, but they're less common.

That being said, there are certain practices and rituals that are considered quite important. In its most basic form, Asatru involves celebrating a few major festivals each year. These festivals occur on the solstices, equinoxes, and the cross-quarter day, although there are a few exceptions to this rule.

Now, when you think of festivals, it would be expected to imagine these large parties that stretch throughout a town and involve the entire community. The Asatru festivals are quite different, and while they are parties, they are often more intimate affairs and are generally held among families or Asatru groups.

Within Asatru, there are two major types of ritual celebrations that are done to honor the Norse pantheon. The first is called the Blot and the second is the Sumbel. There are also numerous social and cultural events that may vary from practitioner to practitioner.

Care for Nature

While not necessarily a key tenet, Asatru does focus on the importance of nature and respecting the environment. Now, as with many aspects of Asatru, this aspect is up for interpretation.

So, what does respecting the environment mean to you?

For some, this could mean starting a community garden or volunteering at an organization focused on conservation and nature. It could mean starting a private garden or caring for plants.

Caring for nature can also be interpreted as caring for wildlife and animals. You could volunteer or work with animals.

Be Careful with Your Words

Within Asatru, words hold power. They matter. The words you speak not only affect you but also the people around you. It is believed that the words you speak also affect your wyrd (your fate or destiny) as well as the wyrd of those around you.

Therefore, words hold immense weight and shouldn't be used carelessly.

The importance of this can be seen in the weight placed on oaths and vows. To break a vow or oath is to dishonor yourself.

Therefore, a good way to practice Asatru is to be careful with your words. Try to be as truthful as you can, don't make promises you can't keep, and don't use your words to hurt others.

How you choose to interpret these suggestions will depend on your own morals and values.

Rituals

Modern rituals are more related to altering a state of awareness to experience different mindsets. The colloquial for this in

North America is a "trance." It can be induced through various elements such as dance, music, chants, and even meditation. Being so absorbed in such a ritual leads people to experience what they describe as "ecstasy." Obviously, people label this feeling as a religious experience and spiritual ecstasy when done in a religious context. At the very forefront of these rituals, there are elements of joy, humor, and happiness and modern Pagans pride themselves on practicing their religion in such a light-hearted, fun manner.

Certain rituals take place within the domestic setting. It can be executed by people individually or even as a family. Primary offerings include bread, cake, and flowers. When you look at it this way, modern Pagan rituals are not very different from traditional paganism. They take inspiration from not only pre-Christian Pagan beliefs but also borrows practices from other religions such as Hinduism, Buddhism, Shinto, Roman Catholicism, and Orthodox Christianity.

Festival

We have already discussed Pagan festivals in detail in earlier chapters. However, it must be noted that there is a shared emphasis on the agricultural cycle and respect for the dead when it comes to modern paganism. The summer solstice and winter solstice are still as important as traditionally and are still the perfect example of Pagan celebrations! The Wheel of Year also plays an integral part in the Pagan festival culture, especially in Wicca.

Magic

Although certain modern Pagans have disassociated themselves from magic and witchcraft, there are quite a handful of them with an ardent belief in the power of magic. However, there is no coherent and shared interpretation of what magic is for modern Pagans. According to Aleister Crowley, magic is the art of causing change to occur "in conformity" with human will. A lot of modern Pagans use this definition to put forth their viewpoints.

The first thing you must do when you get a calling to follow Norse Paganism is to just listen and talk to your gods. Remember that in Heathenism, gods are your friends and kinsfolk, and having conversations with them can build your rapport as well as help you to understand what you need to do and how to move ahead.

An Asatruar's most distinguishing feature is their connection to themselves, their people, and nature. Most Asatruars have deep connections with their respective universes because they were taught to open up and embrace their spirituality. Since heathens are taught to see themselves as powerful beings equal to the Norse gods, they gradually gain the confidence needed to navigate their path in life.

Given the lack of a fixed dogma and the fact that many new believers converted to Norse Paganism from monotheistic religions, there are many interpretations of the Pagan texts and various understandings of several topics, such as how the gods interact with humans and whether or not the Vaettir are considered gods. With all of the differences, there is a sense of mutual respect and understanding of different points of view and interpretations. Asatru priests, on the other hand, are not believed to be inherently better than any other practitioner, but rather as people who have a strong devotion to their religion.

The origin of Asatru is a fascinating story. It is almost unbelievable

CHAPTER 10

Sacred Tools Used to Practice Asatru

that a religion can survive centuries of Christianization behind hidden doors and then make its way out into the modern world centuries later. This only emphasizes the significance and weight of the connection between Norse Paganism and Norse identity. Asatru would not have emerged if there had not been a strong desire among modern people to reconnect with nature and their ancestors' beliefs. The only thing more intriguing is how religion has evolved to adapt to modern times. It is not only interesting from an academic standpoint, but it also demonstrates that Norse Paganism is an ever-changing set of concepts and beliefs, and therefore a living, breathing religion.

Remembering that Paganism encompasses many different traditions—traditions that sometimes have very little in common aside from shared modern history—it is impossible to predict what any Pagan may use in terms of religious tools. Many Pagans will have only a small selection of tools, sticking to what is most relevant to their practice. Not all Pagans practice magick, so these individuals will frequently use fewer tools.

Many of the tools in the following list originated within ceremonial magic and have found their way into the larger Pagan sphere due to the popularity of eclectic Wicca during the nineties. For this reason, some of these tools will be unusual outside of Wiccan or Wiccan-inspired traditions, while some are typical only in religious and secular witchcraft practice.

Sword

Common within ceremonial magic and traditional forms of

Wicca, yet rarely seen outside of them, the sword is a masculine tool corresponding to either fire or air. It is a defensive tool, used for banishing, commanding spirits, and casting the circle (an energetic construct used as part of delineating ritual space).

Pentacle

A small disc made of metal, stone, or wax, the pentacle is inscribed with various symbols, sometimes (but not always) including the symbol of the pentacle. It is a traditional tool of Wicca, used to represent the element of Earth and to consecrate tools and direct energy.

Staff

Found within various Pagan traditions, the staff is a large piece of wood, generally about the height of the person to whom it belongs. It may be carved or decorated. It corresponds to either the fire or the air element.

A bell

It is believed that loud noise drives evil spirits or demons away, which is what the bell is used for in most cases. The vibrations from the bell represent harmony as it includes the shaking of a sistrum, a rattle, or the sound of a "singing bowl." In some religions or practices, the bell is used to start or end a rite, and to call a goddess.

Besom

The besom is a straw broom and is used for sweeping a ceremonial or ritualistic area. Sweeping clears out any negative energy that may exist in the given space. The broom signifies as a purifier so it is linked to the water element.

It is a broom that is used in the cleaning process during a ritual. However, you do not necessarily have to sweep the floor. You can use this tool for a symbolic purpose. When you choose a bosom, see to it that you go for something that is made with natural materials. If you cannot find a besom from a store, you can make your own. Depending on which Wiccan coven or group you belong to, you should follow certain specifications when making your own besom.

Wand

This tool is actually optional. You can choose to have a wand or not. You can buy it from a store or have it custom made. If you choose to have a wand, you can refer to various traditions. In general, a wand has to be the length of your elbows, fingers, and hand, but it can also be twice or half its size. You can choose any material for your wand, but woods are more ideal because they are used by ancient Druids. They are also more connected to nature.

Athame and Sword

An athame is a small knife typically made with wood. It is basically a mini dagger. A sword, on the other hand, is much bigger. It generally comes in a variety of sizes and shapes and is bigger than an athame. You can choose whatever athame or sword best fits your personal preferences. Nonetheless, it is ideal for your athame to be double ended. It also has to have a dark wood on its handle. If you want to personalize it, you can carve symbols on its handle. An athame is a tool many Wiccans and Pagans use for directing energy in their rituals and is often used for casting the Sacred Circle.

Candles

Candles play a major part in any ritual. We have all used the light of candles since we learned how to create our own lasting light and the candle is a great symbol of life in the practice of Wicca.

The act of lighting a candle is a powerful energetic vibration of intention and opens a doorway for you to connect more deeply with the powerful magick you want to invoke. Using candles in all of your ritual and spell work is a good way to bring that energy and focus forward.

Sometimes, you may want to have a candle in a container so that you can burn it overnight or until it burns out. Letting the sacred flame of your spell work continue to burn is a way of energetically stating that your intentions will stay alive until the next candle is lit.

Boline

It is mainly used to cut sacred items that have to be used for rituals and ceremonies. When you use a boline, see to it that you are careful so that you can avoid accidents. You can order this tool online or buy it from a store that sells garden supplies.

Chalice

It is a container used to contain wine, fruit juice, or any other liquid needed for a ritual. You can find chalices in numerous sizes and shapes. Generally, a chalice is simply a cup with a long stem, similar to that of a wine glass. You can get a chalice that is made from any material. Glass and brass are the most commonly used materials for chalices.

Bell

It is used to attract positive energies and invoke deities during rituals. Bells come in different sizes and shapes. They are also widely available, so you can easily purchase them from anywhere. It is up to what kind of bell you will use for your altar. You can use a small one or a big one. You may prefer a small bell since it is easier to hold and has a mild tone.

Cauldron

This tool is perhaps the most associated one with Wicca. It is used to stir and combine ingredients that are used in rituals. As with many of the tools placed on altars, you can find cauldrons in various sizes and shapes. However, you do not have to put your cauldron on your altar if it is too big and heavy. Cauldrons are basically iron pots that have large bottoms and three legs. If your altar is small, you may get a small cauldron that does not take up much space.

Crystal Ball

This tool is used to represent the goddess. Wiccans gaze into their crystal ball to have a vision. You can find crystal balls in different sizes and types. However, once you acquire a crystal ball, make sure that you charge it magically as soon as you can. Crystal balls have long been used in witchcraft and other similar practices.

Stones and Crystals

Stones and crystals, as you read about briefly in the above list of tools, each have unique qualities and characteristics. Some of them are good for protection and grounding, while others are best for enhancing the connection with spirit and opening the third eye.

Try an experiment to find the right stones and crystals: find a local shop in your area that specializes in selling stones and crystals. While in the shop, use your dominant magick hand (it might not be your dominant writing hand) and hover over the stones you feel drawn to. Let your intuition be your guide. If you feel "pulled" toward a stone, pick it up and notice how it feels. If you can sense a strong energy in it through the palm of your hand, then that stone or crystal is resonating with your vibration and will be good for you to work with.

Sensor

This tool is used to hold the incense that you burn during your rituals. You can find sensors in different sizes, shapes, and materials. They are typically made of brass. Nonetheless, you may also use a hanging sensor or a glass tray if it is more convenient for you. A hanging sensor is actually ideal if you wish to disperse the smoke from your incense during your ritual sessions.

Altar Tile

This tool is used as the central area during the ritual process and may contain a pentagram. It is available in different materials. Your altar tile can be of any size, but it is better to have one that fits your altar perfectly.

Clothing

You are allowed to wear whatever you want during a ritual, provided that it is approved by the members of your coven. If you are a solitary practitioner, you can wear whatever you want as long as you feel comfortable in it. You should be able to easily stand up, sit down, and move around. Most Wiccans wear robes that feature embroidery, hoods, and flared sleeves. If you are not comfortable wearing a robe, you can wear something casual such as a pair of jeans and a T-shirt. You can even be nude if you like.

Jewelry and Accessories

The use of jewelry and accessories is open to many different interpretations. Wiccans are not really required to wear jewelry during a ritual. However, if you wish to wear any celestial

CHAPTER 11

THE SIGNIFICANCE OF THE AFTERLIFE

symbol or an amulet, you can wear it. You may also wear a bracelet or a ring that features a special gem or stone.

Smudging Stick

When you use a smudge stick in your spells and rituals, you are energetically purifying the space around you and protecting your energy from unwanted energies that may be drawn to you. You can use the smoke of your smudge stick to draw a wide circle around the space you will be casting in. You can also use salt in the same way, but often the mess is harder to clean up, unless you are outside.

The Old Norse religion has fully developed concepts of the afterlife. According to Sturluson, there are four realms that the dead people are welcomed into. Interestingly, Norse Paganism did not believe that the morals followed in human life would impact the individual's destination to his or her afterlife.

Warriors who died in battle were taken to Valhalla, Odin's hall, where they waited until Ragnarok when they would battle with the Æsir. Those who died from old age or disease would go to Hel. The other two afterlife realms mentioned by Sturluson were the hall of Brimir and the hall of Sindri. Some Eddic poems talk of the dead living in their graves, remaining conscious there.

The Norse god Odin is most closely associated with death, especially death by hanging. There is a reference to Odin in *The Poetic Edda* to this effect. Odin hanged himself on Yggdrasil for nine nights to gain magical power and wisdom.

The Norse didn't really have a well-defined sense of the afterlife. Some sources claim that the spirit goes on to a spirit hall such as Valhalla or even Hel's Hall upon death. In the world of the dead, the spirits did the same things they did in real life. They dueled, drank and ate, and they continued to practice their magic. It's not quite clear how a soul was picked to go to Valhalla or Helheim, but the choice seemed to have something to do with whether the dead were warriors or lived plain lives.

The warriors went to Valhalla if they died honorably in battle. Those who died without a sword in their hands were probably sent to Helheim. This might also be why Viking warriors were buried with their swords in their hands as part of their funeral rites. Historians quickly point out that we only have this distinction between Valhalla and Helheim due to the early Christian scholar Snorri Sturluson who recorded most of the Viking myths and runes in the *Poetic Edda*. There was also a belief among early Vikings that the dead can be reborn into a relative. Thus, when Thor died, he could have been reborn into one of his sons. This is quite likely as there are some accounts of Viking myth that indicate the fallen gods would be reborn again.

Lastly, there is also no concept of punishment or reward for life in death with the Vikings. They didn't believe you went to Helheim as punishment or to Valhalla as a reward. Instead, it was simply another place to exist in. The idea of heaven and hell was very Christian and didn't feature in Viking myth until much later in Norse history when Christianity had begun pollinating Norse culture with biblical beliefs.

Hel, the Ruler of Helheim and the Realm of the Dead

Hel was the daughter of Loki and the giantess Angrboda, and her name hints at her dark persona as the meaning of Hel is "hidden." She is described as having a face that is half healthy and fleshy colored, and half rotten and skeletal.

Like the underworld or Helheim—hidden realm—that she governs, Hel is not a friendly person. She is 100 percent giant, which leaves no doubt where her allegiances lie during Ragnarok. With a giant wolf and a monstrous sea serpent as siblings, this makes for a rather strange and fiendish family. As we would imagine the ruler of the underworld to be, Hel is not a charitable or kind deity. She is rather obsessed with her own goals and her dark purposes of gathering up a host of the dead to fight in the final days of Ragnarok.

Helheim is populated by all people who died of sickness or disease or old age. Only warriors who die in battle can progress up Yggdrasil to reach Valhalla. The rest go down to Helheim. The journey to Helheim is not one that is pleasant or easy. To reach the hall of Hel, one has to travel for nine days and nights through a desolate landscape where the path is known to cut feet to shreds.

Then, cross the dangerous river Gjoll with a glass bridge suspended by strings of hair. Falling into the river is best avoided as there are knives floating in the tumultuous waters. The bridge is also guarded by a terrifying giantess, Modgud, whose name doesn't inspire friendly chatter. Her name, meaning "furious battle," clearly announces what will happen to those who dare enter without permission or purpose.

The palace in Helheim is surrounded by a tall wall, which has a single gate to allow the dead to enter. Hel rules in the halls of her kingdom as queen of the dead. True to form, all the objects in her hall have misfortunate names. The large table is called hunger, while the knives and forks are called starvation. Her bedroom is equally depressing, and her bed is known as a sickbed, while the surrounding curtains are called misfortune.

When Hel went collecting the dead on Earth/Midgard, she used a rake to choose who she would take to Helheim, but when there was an outbreak of pestilence, she used a broom, simply sweeping the dead into her kingdom. While the Christian concept of hell is not pleasant, involving torture by terrifying demons, the Norse idea of Helheim wasn't all that bad. When Baldur arrived in Helheim, he was welcomed with a feast of freshly cooked foods, and even Hel herself sat him next to her in her hall.

CHAPTER 12

Get to Know the Asatru and Norse Symbols

Hel's Role in Baldur's Remaining Unresurrected

While the story about Baldur's death is more about Loki, we do see some aspects of Hel's character in it, too. When Hermod rode into Helheim to ask for Baldur's resurrection, Hel showed little concern for the worlds beyond her own realm. She seemed to have utter disregard for what Baldur's death meant for the end of days. The deal she offered, that every living being in the cosmos must weep for Baldur, was hardly a fair one, especially since her own father was a being in that cosmos, and Loki had been the one who orchestrated Baldur's death.

Within Paganism you'll find a considerable variety of symbols. Many of these symbols were originally found in ancient cultures, while others are modern. There is no one tradition within Paganism that incorporates all of these symbols, and some are exclusive to certain traditions. Solitary eclectic Pagans tend to make use of symbols as they hold relevance within their practice, to the gods they honor, and to any magick they may be working, so their use of symbols may be very fluid and situationally dependent.

Pentacle

A five-pointed star (pentagram) bound by a circle, the pentacle is an ancient symbol found in many different cultures and religions, including Christianity. It is apotropaic, meaning it is a symbol of protection. It is also the generally recognized symbol of Wicca, relating to the element of Earth.

Gungnir

The Gungnir symbol is also known as the Spear of Odin and the Sword of Odin. It symbolizes the legendary weapon of Odin called the Gungnir. The Dwarves crafted this weapon. Gungnir was acquired by Loki and was given to Odin. The Gungnir never misses where it aims and always returns to the hand of Odin.

Triple Moon

With two crescent moons on either side of a circle, the triple moon symbol represents the lunar cycle in the northern hemisphere (as it shows the waxing, full, and waning phases) as well as goddesses associated with the moon. It can be used to draw in lunar energies or to help with focus in working with lunar deities.

Vegvisir

This symbol may or may not be a true symbol of Norse origin, but it was found in a manuscript with magical significance, and so it is included here. The idea was that this symbol could help you find your way if you are lost. This applies to feeling both spiritually and figuratively and physically lost. It is considered a magical compass or a runic compass. It was believed to provide guidance for anyone who'd lost or might lose their way and was drawn on ships during the Viking period to ensure a safe return home.

Eye of Horus

Also known as the Wadjet, the Egyptian eye of Horus is depicted as a right eye. It is associated with protection, the lunar-associated god Horus, good health, and power.

Helm of Awe

Like Thor's Hammer, the Helm of Awe is seen as a protective symbol. It also symbolizes strength, but it has a darker aspect than the hammer, at least depending on the individual use. It is a rune stave. The original name, Aegishjalmur, comes from two different Old Norse words, "shield" (aegis) and "Hjalmr" (helm).

Eye of Ra

Similar to the eye of Horus, the eye of Ra is depicted as a left eye. It is associated with the solar-aligned god Ra, good fortune, and creation.

Mjölnir

This is Thor's Hammer, said in cosmology to be crafted in the fiery forges of the dwarves. It was a symbol of protection and integrity and tradition, strength, custom, and consecration. Considered a tool rather than a weapon, it may be the most important symbol in Norse culture. In the Old Norse language, Mjölnir meant "lightning" or white like the color of lighting or pure snow. The word may also mean "to crush." (Mythologian, n.d.) Mjölnir was also worn to provide protection in battle. This lasted even after Christianity was introduced.

Ankh

A cross with the upper vertical bar formed as a loop, the Egyptian ankh represents life and the power to maintain and restore life. It sometimes represents air and breath (especially as in "the breath of life").

Hekate's Wheel

Also known as the strophalos, Hekate's wheel is a common symbol among devotees of the goddess Hekate, representing her as a triform goddess (not a triple goddess). It is used as a focal point in rituals, as part of evoking Her in workings, and as a representation of one's devotion to Her.

Valknut

Associated with the god Odin, as well as with a transition from life to death and death itself, Valknut has a darker cast, but was also used in Norse magic. It may also be called Odin's knot, Hrungnir's heart, or the slain warrior's heart. Symbolically, it uses three triangles. Because of that, Valknut is said to resemble the three roots of Yggdrasil, the tree that led to all creation. These three roots lead to three of the main realms created from the great tree: Asgard, the home of the gods; Jotunheim, the realm of giants; and Niflheim, the underworld. As there are three vertices per triangle and the triangles interlock, they could also represent all nine of the realms and the way in which they are interconnected. (Mythologian, n.d.)

Triquetra

Also called a trefoil knot or trinity knot, the triquetra originated among Celtic people, likely in the seventh century. In modern Paganism, it is used to represent feminine deities; land, sky, and sea; and the modern concept of maiden, mother, and crone as used by Dianic Wiccans.

Triskele

Comprised of three interlocking spirals, the triskele is an ancient Celtic symbol representing movement and motion, especially cycles. Modern Pagans may also use it to represent the three levels of the self; land, sky, and sea; and any other particular meaningful association with the number three.

Septagram

A seven-pointed star, it is sometimes called an elven or faery star. Its seven points are given a variety of associations, particularly the seven directions (north, east, south, west, above, below, and within) and the seven planets.

Spiral Goddess

A modern symbol representing divine feminine energy, the spiral goddess taps into the procreative powers associated with women who menstruate. The spiral on the belly is indicative of the creative powers of the uterus as connected to pregnancy. It is a favored symbol among feminist witches and Pagans.

Labyrinth

An ancient symbol of various forms, the labyrinth combines the wholeness of the circle with the inward/outward movement of the spiral. In Paganism, it can be used to enter a trance state, by walking a labyrinth, or by tracing a small labyrinth with one finger or a stylus. It is especially useful for finding answers to problems by seeking a way through the maze.

Air

The alchemical symbol for air is frequently used to represent the element of air. It is depicted as a masculine, upward-pointing triangle bisected by a horizontal line. This symbol allows you to tap into the elemental qualities of air: intellect, communication, and travel.

Earth

Depicted as a feminine, downward-pointing triangle bisected by a horizontal line, the alchemical symbol for Earth is often used to represent the element of Earth and to tap into its qualities of strength, stability, and constancy.

Troll Cross

The troll cross is an ornament made of a single rod of iron crossed at the base (perhaps in the symbolism of an odal rune). It is believed to be a charm worn by Scandinavians as security against trolls and other evil mythical beings. Both iron and crosses were both accepted to protect people from malicious creatures.

Fire

In alchemy, the element of fire is depicted as a masculine, upward-pointing triangle. This symbol is common throughout Paganism. It is used as a simple means of tapping into the transformative and protective qualities of the fire element.

Triceps

It is another common version of the Valknut; it resembles a cut-away triangle or a triangle formed of three diamonds (three 'othala' runes interwoven).

It was used as a magical sign of protection into the middle ages. The othala rune signifies the home and one's ancestors.

Water

A feminine, downward-pointing triangle, this symbol also comes to Paganism from alchemy. It is an effective way to tap into the water element's qualities of fluidity and psychicness.

Shield Knot

This symbol is also known as the Four Corners and the Quaternary Knot. The shield knot is an artifact from the ancient world and is nearly universal. The shield image has been utilized for many years by an assortment of societies for security and warding. While the knotwork shield is frequently connected with the Celts and Old Norse, the essential frame is much more old-fashioned.

Its origins can be tracked down as far back as Mesopotamia, which the symbol there was connected with defensive spells summoning the divine forces of the four corners of the earth.

Later, the four-corners insignia was utilized as a part of the Kabbalah as an image of the Shema, the petition/spell to summon the four Archangels; it is the beginning of the "Qabbalistic Cross" custom still utilized as a part of enchantment today.

Horned God

A circle topped with an upward-pointing crescent, the horned god symbol is modern, coming into Paganism from Wicca, where it represents the masculine deity. It is a symbol of divine masculine energy and the creative, protective, and wild energies often associated with such traits.

Helm of Awe (Ægishjálmr)

An ancient Germanic symbol, the helm of awe is a symbol of protection and power, believed to be able to strike adversaries with terror so as to prevent them from attacking. It is often used in Paganism as a symbol of physical, mental, and spiritual protection.

Swastika

We must now take a look at the infamous swastika symbol. This symbol is a very powerful image. It is why the nazis chose it and that is why the image provokes taboos of the modern age. Despite this, the swastika is an image found in all religions on earth. It shows up on each continent and is as old as mankind and the beginnings of civilization thereof. A marker of the sun's ventures can be seen on Pictish shake carvings, embellishing old Greek stoneware, and on antiquated Norse weapons and other relics.

Swastikas were etched onto various cave walls in France around 5000 B.C. Away from Europe, a swastika denoted the start of numerous Buddhist sacred writings and is still regularly chiseled on the soles of the feet of the Buddha in statuary. In the Jain religion, this symbol is an image of the seventh Jina (Saint), the Tirthankara Suparsva. To Native Americans, the swastika is an image of the sun, the four headings, and the four seasons.

Geometrically, the swastika is a solar symbol, with its arms bowed at right points, recommending a spinning or turning movement.

The name swastika is gotten from the Sanskrit dialect, from "su," signifying "great," and "vasti," signifying "being" (as one: prosperity). In India, it is utilized as a fruitfulness and rabbit's foot. The correct turning Indian swastika symbolizes the sun and positive vitality and is most normally connected with Ganesh, a god of flourishing and riches.

Tree of Life

A common symbol throughout many ancient cultures, the tree of life is also known as the world tree and by the name Yggdrasil in Heathenry. Its meanings are varied, representing a connective force linking the physical world and the spirit world, immortality, and fertility.

Solar Cross

The Solar Cross is also known to some by the additional names of Odin's Cross, the Sun Cross, or the Wheel of Taranis.

The Solar Cross is probably one of the oldest religious symbols in the world. It has made historical appearances in Asia,

America, Europe, and India. It is embedded in the sacred art of all these continents from the very dawn of human history. It consists of a very simple design. It is composed of an equal-armed cross within a circle.

Each quadrant represents the four equal parts of the solar calendar—Summer, Fall, Winter, and Spring. Additionally, the arms point to specific positions of the sun in the year, known to us by the name of the solstices. The infamous symbol of the Swastika is also a valid form of the Solar cross, albeit with a slightly different meaning.

Rod of Asclepius

Originating in ancient Greece, this symbol depicts the rod held by the god Asclepius. It is frequently confused with the caduceus. A rod with a single snake twined about it, the rod of Asclepius represents medicine and healing.

Odin's Horns

The Triple Horn of Odin is an adapted symbol of the Norse God Odin. This image comprises three interlocked drinking horns and is usually worn or shown as an indication of responsibility to the present-day Asatru religion. The horns figure in the legendary stories of Odin and are utilized in traditional Norse toasting ceremonies and everyday use.

Most stories include the god's mission for the Odhroerir, a supernatural mead blended from the blood of the insightful god Kvasir. However, the stories often have variations; Odin utilizes his mind and enchantment to acquire the blend more than three days; the three horns mirror the three drafts of the supernatural mead.

Caduceus

Often confused with the rod of Asclepius, the caduceus is a rod twined with two serpents and sometimes depicted with wings at the top, carried by the god Hermes. It is associated with commerce and business.

Ouroboros

Depicted as a snake (sometimes a dragon) eating its own tail and forming a circle, this symbol is common within Western esotericism. It represents wholeness, eternity, and the cycle of life, death, and rebirth.

Thor's Hammer (Mjölnir)

A Norse symbol found within modern Heathenry, Mjölnir is the war hammer carried by the god Thor. It is a symbol of protection and is also used to denote a devotee of Thor, in addition to being used as a representative symbol of Heathenry in general.

Spiral

The spiral is an ancient symbol found in numerous cultures. In modern Paganism, it represents creative energy, movements, and cycles. It is often used in magick to draw energy in or send it out, depending on whether the spiral is drawn in a clockwise or counterclockwise direction.

Awen

The representative symbol of modern Druidry, the Awen symbolizes divine inspiration. It is a modern symbol, and its three lines are also viewed as representing the three domains of land, sky, and sea.

Irminsul

The Irminsul was an ancient pillar that was the hub of religious worship by the Anglo Saxons. Charlemagne decimated in 772 A.D, who waged war against the pagans for over 30 years. The Irminsul meaning and purpose have become obscured through

CHAPTER 13

The Sacred Asatru Calendar and Holidays

the sands of time, but it is undoubtedly associated with the Anglo-Saxon god Irmin.

It has been declared that this god is identical to the Nordic God Tyr. Some historians have asserted that the Irminsul is a physical construction of the World Tree Yggdrasil. Its esoteric meaning is the world cross, which has been said to be the image of man and the universe or the crossing of physical reality with that of the spiritual realm. It is the marriage of the two.

Celebrations and festivals are an integral part of Heathenism, and the Heathen calendar is replete with feast days, memorial days, and other special occasions. In fact, keeping and performing festivals is one of the primary duties of an Asatruar. Keeping these important days reflects the respect and love for their ancestors, gods, and goddesses.

Celebrating festivals and commemorating our ancestors and gods fills us with a deep sense of sacredness and takes us closer to the spirits of our ancestors and our deities. When we remember them on special days, they return the gift by providing us with protection, strength, and courage.

Most of our festival and feast days are aligned with the agricultural patterns of our culture and tradition, which, in turn, align our lives with the dynamism of climate and weather changes. Accordingly, every festival, feast, and ritual represents a transformation of the Earth as well as our souls.

Asatru has a compilation of all the feasts and festivals of all the Germanic and Nordic tribes that were considered important right throughout Northern Europe. In ancient times, some tribes kept certain feasts while others kept other festivals. The important thing about festivals in Asatru is not the time or even the ritual. It is more about the gods, goddesses, and ancestors who are hailed and worshipped as the Earth transforms around us. Let us look at some traditional festivals of Asatru in detail, although a couple of them were discussed briefly in the previous chapter.

Disting

Each year, on February 2, Norse people celebrate the female ancestral spirits, the souls of the women of their family tree from its beginning. It's said that these women still continue to watch over the younger generations, and with Frigga's help, they will continue to do so. Besides them, other Nordic gods are also honored during this time. Some of them are deep winter figures like Ullr, Skadi, and Rind. Others are more associated with warmth, as is Logi, a fire giant, or Glut, along with her daughters Einmyria and Eisa. Mengloth, Eir, and their maidens are also often honored at this time for helping to heal communal illnesses, which are usually at their worst during winter. Additionally, some people may offer thanks to Bragi for creating poetry to chase away boredom on long winter days.

Disting is not only known for being associated with snow and cold but also with healing. On this day, there is often a group of people singing around a fire hearth trying to help the spiritual warming of those who need it. Another thing that's commonly done on this day is land preparation for planting and growing crops and the accounting of one's wealth. If someone came into possession of something that made them richer on this very day, it was viewed as the sign of prosperity that was sure to come later in the year.

Ostara—March 20th–21st

The Ostara signifies the Spring Equinox and is celebrated on March 21 every year. Marking the start of the summer months, it is named after the goddess Ostara, an important Germanic deity who embodied spring and the renewal and revival of life. The name Ostara signifies the east and glory.

The Ostara festival is a celebration of the revival of the Earth after months of freezing cold winters. Traditionally, homes are decorated with flowered, colored eggs, budding boughs, branches, etc. The hare was the spirit animal or holy beast of the goddess Ostara. Slaying and eating rabbit meat was permitted only after taking permission from the goddess.

Holding and keeping the Ostara feast enhances the joy and happiness of the festival participants.

Some common folklore traditions that have carried on from ancient times and continue even today include:

- Fires kindled at the top of hills at the break of dawn.
- The performance of plays in villages and rural areas. In these plays, summer and winter are shown as people battling with each other, with summer winning over winter and driving him off of the stage.
- Effigies signify winter as drowned, beaten, and burned to indicate the end of winter.

Lithasblot

Urda, the goddess of harvest and her magic that made it possible for the year's bounty, is celebrated with Lithasblot, a ceremony held between July 31 and August 1. In the lives of Old Norse folk, this was the time when the first fruits of the harvest were brought to the gods as gifts. The First Sheaf was bound and blessed as an offering to deities at the beginning of harvest. Putting up decoration around wells and natural springs was often made at this time, a custom, which survived until modern times. Aside from this, the feast of thanksgiving for bread is also quite common. During this, the bread is baked into the shape of Frey, and then broken into pieces. Finally, it's shared amongst all of those who celebrate this holiday together.

Midsummer

On June 20, when the Sun's power is at its utmost height, the celebration of the Midsummer Blot (or Summer Solstice) begins. Although lasting only two days, this is a very eventful holiday during which many trades and connections are made. It also serves as an occasion to celebrate all the successful expeditions, hunting, and fishing trips done during the whole summer. Midsummer also signifies the end of all things positives, as it's held on the longest day of the year from which things are said to get more difficult as the days shorten.

While nowadays summer is often taught to begin with the Summer Solstice, according to Old Norse traditions, this is actually the time when this season starts to end. This is possibly due to the death of the Fair God of sunshine, Baldur, which happened at the turning point at which summer reached its height. For this reason, it's believed that when the Sun shines longest is when the days will soon begin to shorten. The Earth begins its inevitable descent into the cold season of winter. Along with Baldur, Midsummer is also a time to celebrate Sunna. The union of Frey and Freya and their combined energies are said to make the flowers turn to fruit if asked by followers during the festivities. At the height of the summer, Heimdall and his rainbow bridge are often visible. Because of this, it's often honored at this time as well.

Yule or Yuletide—The 12-Day Festival

The festival of Yule starts approximately on December 20th and goes on until the beginning of the next year. The word Yule is derived from "hjol," an Old Norse language term meaning "wheel." This is the period when the year's wheel is at its lowest point and is set to rise again.

"Hjol" or wheel is a direct reference to the Sun as a fiery wheel that rolls across the sky. It is important to note here that Yuletide celebrations predate Christmas and Christianity by thousands of years. Ancient Icelandic sagas are replete with references to Yuletide and also have descriptions of how this festival was celebrated. Yuletide was a time of joy, festivities, exchanging gifts, dancing, and singing.

The holidays of Yuletide were considered to be the most sacred amongst all ancient Germanic tribes. According to Norse Paganism, this period marks the return of Balder from Helheim. It also marks the beginning of the end of freezing winters. The start of the Yuletide festival has no fixed date. But it is typically celebrated for twelve days and usually begins at sunset on the day of the Winter Solstice (the longest night and the shortest day of the year), which normally falls on December 20th in the Northern Hemisphere.

The first night of the Yuletide is called Mother's Night when Frigg and female ancestor spirits (collectively called Disir) are honored. The name also refers to the rebirth of the world from the darkness of winter. A nightlong traditional vigil is kept on Mother's Night to make sure that the Sun will rise again after the darkest night and to warmly welcome it.

Walpurgis

The festival of Walpurgis is held between April 22 and 30, in commemoration of Odin's sacrifice that was made on April 30. On this day, the Allfather had hung for nine days on the World Tree, gained the wisdom of the Runes, and died for a brief moment. All of the light in the nine worlds went out as a result of this, and chaos ensued. Therefore, this festival represents a significant period of darkness. However, at midnight, the light returned, signaling the reverence of the new beginning. The last day of April is also a day of celebration of Freya, the goddess of love, and Lofn and Sjofn, other minor love goddesses. Frey is often honored with establishing a Maypole, along with Var to whom people pledge oaths at the said pole. The Maypole is traditionally carried around in procession, making it possible for everyone to see it and ask for help if needed.

Winter Nights

Despite signifying the beginning of the unforgiving Winter Season, Winter nights are often characterized as a ceremony of wild abandon. Here, one's ancestors are celebrated and asked for help or advice regarding the coming year. This festival, which runs from October 29 to November 1, is thought to be a time to foretell the fates of many people. Animals that were not expected to survive the winter were frequently used for these purposes. They are sacrificed for the community's benefit and to ward off evil spirits. Unlike many other rituals, this is often done by the woman of a family. She is considered the ultimate keeper of the house and her family. So this way, she can protect her entire home.

On this day, Hela, the goddess of the Dead, and Mordgud, the guardian of the Underworld, are honored as new rulers of the ancestors. Nidhogg, the corpse-eating dragon, was asked to spare them, while Hlin, the goddess of Grief, and Hermod, the messenger of the gods, who walked the road to Hel, were also asked to assist in providing comfort to both the living and the dead. Another common way to celebrate this festival was the hallowing and leaving of the Last Sheaf in the field for Odin to find it. He can then bring it with him in Wild Hunt when he is battling ghosts and other spirits after Winter nights. By leaving the fields to him, people are able to do some self-reflection and contemplate their actions from the passing year, so they can make better ones in the next one.

Mabon

Being a minor blot, Mabon or Haustblot has fewer records of being celebrated than many others. According to some traditions, it's held around the 22nd of September and represents the end of the harvest season. At this time, people were (and in agricultural communities still are) too busy with collecting and storing their harvest. This means that they didn't have time to prepare full feasts like for other festivities. But they did have smaller-sized sacred ritual feasts, which were made to honor the gods of food harvest—Frey, Nerthus, Iduna, and Njord. Jord was once again given thanks for all her contributions, along with Snotra, goddess of hard work and hospitality. Huldra, the keeper of flocks, is also honored for making it possible to raise the animals and have enough meat and other animal products for the colder months.

For the Asatruar, this is still a joyous festival, which is celebrated by building bonfires, feasting, and dancing on the Autumn Equinox. Having lit these fires as their only light source, families and whole pagan communities often gather and bond together by telling old tales over the flame. Traditionally, this is done to avoid being alone and missing since this was considered dangerous because it meant that the person was exposed to the dangers of the coming season. As the second harvest festival of the season, Mabon is also a time to find reasons to be thankful and celebrate surviving another season of hard work. By gathering into masses, people are able to do all this together, strengthening the spirit of the community.

Fall Feast

Also known as Haustblot. This occasion falls on the autumn equinox and is the start of autumn in the northern hemisphere. Like Midsummer, this is a joyous time with bonfires, feasting, and dancing to mark the occasion. Previously, villages would throw bones from slaughtered cattle into the fire. With a large bonfire burning, the villagers would extinguish any other fire. Each family would then light their hearth from the one bonfire, bonding all the families together.

Practically, this time marked the beginning of gathering food for the long winter days ahead. In modern times, the importance of this festival has been curtailed for most people. From an agricultural standpoint, for those of whom a difficult season would mean a long winter of famine, this time was of the utmost importance.

The Holy Days

The Asatru calendar has a number of holy days. In February, on the 2nd is the event of Bari. On this day, the wooing of Ingvi Freyr is celebrated. This day is a festival of fertility. The 9th and the 14th are also significant, but the 14th is not associated with the modern Valentine's Day holiday. Instead, the Feast of Vali takes place. The rest of the months contain several holy days.

Thorrablot

An Icelandic holiday with Viking roots, this holiday is still celebrated by some in Iceland. It is seen as a cultural celebration; however, for the heathens, this holiday is a time to celebrate Thor or the winter spirit Thorri or both.

This holiday was a sacrificial festival offered to the gods. It was then abolished as Iceland was Christianized but brought back to life during the 19th century. On this holiday, a blot is dedicated to Thor, believed to protect humans from the Frost Giants.

A feast is laid out, and following dinner, group games are played and singing, storytelling, and drinking. The dancing then

REFERENCES

begins and usually continues until the early morning when the holiday celebrations end.

With all Asatru holidays and celebrations, there are many ways to celebrate. From prayers to a blot, this is a time to honor Thor for all of the gifts and bounties he gives to human beings.

Asatru Alliance. (n.d.). Retrieved from Asatru.org website: https://www.asatru.org/aboutasatru.php

Asatru, An Ancient Religion Reborn. (n.d.). Retrieved from Irminsul.org website: http://www.irminsul.org/arc/016pb.html

Groeneveld, E. (2017). Norse Mythology. World History Encyclopedia. Retrieved from https://www.worldhistory.org/Norse_Mythology/

Norse Mythology 101—An Introduction to our Viking Myths books. (n.d.). Retrieved from Salariya.com website: https://www.salariya.com/article/norse-mythology-101-introduction-our-viking-myths-books Norse mythology for Smart People—the ultimate online guide to Norse mythology and religion. (2012, November 14). Retrieved from Norse-mythology.org website: https://norse-mythology.org/

Scott, J. (2020, December 3). A beginner's guide to Norse mythology—life in Norway. Retrieved from Lifeinnorway.net website: https://www.lifeinnorway.net/norse-mythology/

Asatru Alliance. (n.d.). Retrieved from Asatru.org website:

https://www.asatru.org/roleofgothar.php

ASATRU (Norse Heathenism). (n.d.). Retrieved from Religioustolerance.org website: https://www.religioustolerance.org/asatru.htm

Blain, J., & Wallis, R. J. (2009). Heathenry. In Handbook of Contemporary Paganism (pp. 413–432). BRILL.

Íslenska Ásatrúarfélagið. (n.d.). Retrieved from En-academic.com website: https://en-academic.com/dic.nsf/enwiki/1198846

Loki. (n.d.). Retrieved from Mythopedia.com website: https://mythopedia.com/norse-mythology/gods/loki/

The Editors of Encyclopedia Britannica. (2021). Odin. In Encyclopedia Britannica.

Thor. (n.d.). Retrieved from Mythopedia.com website: https://mythopedia.com/norse-mythology/gods/thor/

Wigington, P. (n.d.). What is the Asatru Pagan Tradition? Retrieved from Learnreligions.com website: https://www.learnreligions.com/asatru-modern-paganism-2562545

(N.d.). Retrieved from Icelandmag. is website: https://icelandmag.is/article/11-things-know-about-present-day-practice-asatru-ancient-religion-vikings Oertel, K. (Ed.). (2015). Ásatrú: Die Rückkehr der Götter (3rd ed.). Remda-Teichel, Germany: Edition Roter Drache.

WHAT IS ASATRU? (n.d.). Retrieved from Odinsvolk.ca website: http://www.odinsvolk.ca/O.V.A.%20-%20ASATRU%20INTRO.htm

Ecer. (2010, September 30). Nine noble virtues of Ásatrú. Retrieved from Ecer-org.eu website: https://ecer-org.eu/nine-noble-virtues-of-asatru/

NINE NOBLE VIRTUES of ASATRU. (n.d.). Retrieved from Odinsvolk.ca website: http://www.odinsvolk.ca/O.V.A.%20-%20NNV.htm

Wigington, P. (n.d.). The Nine Noble Virtues of Asatru. Retrieved from Learnreligions.com website: https://www.learnreligions.com/noble-virtues-of-asatru-2561539

ASATRU (Norse Heathenism). (n.d.). Retrieved from Religioustolerance.org website: https://www.religioustolerance.org/asatru.htm

Black, J. (2020, June 25). The story of Ragnarok, the ancient Norse Apocalypse. *Ancient Origins*. https://www.ancient-origins.net/myths-legends/story-ragnarok-and-apocalypse-001352

Fenrir. (2012, November 15). Norse mythology for smart people. https://norse-mythology.org/gods-and-creatures/giants/fenrir/

Foster, J. (2020, August 31). Fossegrim and His Fiddle: The Troll at the Heart of Norwegian Music—The American Skald. *Jameson Foster*. https://www.theamericanskald.com/blog/fossegrim

Fuglesang, S. H. (1989). Viking and Medieval Amulets in Scandinavia. Forvännen(84), pp. 15–25.

Geller, P. (2016, October 15). *Ratatoskr*. Mythology. https://mythology.net/norse/norse-creatures/ratatoskr/

Glosecki, S. O. (1989). Shamanism and Old English Poetry.

Printed in Great Britain
by Amazon